Into the New Age

Stephen Verney studied at Balliol, Oxford and Westcott House Theological College, Cambridge. During the war he served with the Friends' Ambulance Unit and later, as a member of the Intelligence Corps, worked with the Greek Resistance in Crete.

Since he was ordained, he has worked in a suburb, on a council housing estate, in a rural parish, at a cathedral at the heart of an industrial city, and now at a national centre in Windsor Castle.

As Canon Residentiary of Coventry Cathedral he was responsible for bringing together representatives of thirty-three nations in a conference 'People and Cities', to search for a positive vision of the city of the future.

Now, in the College of St George at Windsor, he shares responsibility for the worship of the famous Chapel with its ancient musical traditions, and for the training of clergy and laity to take part in the renewal of the Church in the last quarter of the twentieth century.

Stephen Verney

INTO THE NEW AGE

Fontana/Collins

First published in Fontana 1976
© Stephen Verney 1976

Made and printed in Great Britain by
William Collins Sons & Co Ltd Glasgow

A design for a crucifix on which
Scilla Verney was working at the
time of her death.

Acknowledgements

The author and publisher would like to acknowledge their gratitude for permission to quote from 'Four Quartets' from *Collected Poems 1909-1962* by T. S. Eliot published by Faber and Faber Ltd.

The biblical quotations are taken from the New English Bible, second edition © 1970 by permission of Oxford and Cambridge University Presses.

Contents

Foreword

There can be little doubt that we stand on the edge of a new epoch. Old patterns of behaviour are breaking up, and by the end of the twentieth century our way of life will be very different. Anyone who dares to think and to feel at such a time must be looking towards the future with a mixture of terror and hope.

I believe that we could enter the new age for good rather than for ill through the discovery of *interdependence*. We are part of nature, of each other, and of God. We are more earthy, and more heavenly, than we have cared to admit.

But this discovery is painful and dangerous. We become aware that good and evil are interlocked in everybody and everything, and chiefly within ourselves. As we uncover our potentialities for good, we uncover at the same time our potentialities for evil. Is there any way out of this tragic predicament?

The answer to that question is the central theme of this book, and it began to reveal itself to me in the act of writing. One day, I found myself looking with surprise at some words I had written about the coming of the new age . . . 'good and evil interlocked, and transformed by death and resurrection'. This way of death and resurrection, I now see, is the way we have to go.

There is nothing new about *saying* this. What we need, in the crisis of this generation, is new courage in *choosing* it, new depth in *feeling* it, and a new perspective in *understanding* it. I was helped towards the threshold of such an understanding by personal experience. This book was begun in the corridor of a cancer ward in a London hospital, and was finished six months to the day after the death of my wife. Personal, social and spiritual levels of understanding have cross-fertilized, and I hope that they may have given birth to an idea which springs out of the wholeness of human life and points along the way 'into the new age'.

The title of this book is a translation of some Greek words, *eis ton aiona* (literally=into the aeon), which occur like a refrain through St John's gospel. Some examples of their use are listed on page 10. They tell us about the new age and about the way into it, but also about the pioneer who has already explored the way and opened up the new age, and who will be with us through the difficulties and dangers of our own journey.

I believe they point towards the mystery of resurrection, and towards a new possibility of being human. So in spite of the dangers of the way, I offer you this book with a certain light-heartedness, and in the hope that it may be for you a signpost towards the ultimate joy.

Graffham, Sussex
Easter Monday, 1975

Jesus offers water – if you drink it, you will not thirst 'into the new age'.

He offers bread – if you eat it, you will live 'into the new age'.

He offers truth – if you keep it, you will no longer be slaves but you will be free, like sons living in their father's house 'into the new age'.

Jesus is the good shepherd – whose sheep will not perish 'into the new age'.

He is the resurrection – those who believe in him will not die 'into the new age'.

He is the Christ, the king of the new age – who abides (survives) 'into the new age'.

He washes his disciples' feet 'into the new age'.

He gives the Spirit, which will be with them 'into the new age'.

(The Gospel according to St John)

Part I

THE LEAP

1. *The Search for the Holy Grail*

The human race is approaching an evolutionary leap forward in the realm of the spirit and at the same time is being swept towards catastrophe. This is the crisis for our generation.

The purpose of this book is to explore the nature of the evolutionary leap, and to describe both *what* the new age looks like as it begins to emerge, and *how* we may hope to enter it.

Only a tiny fraction of that purpose can be achieved by one book or one author. The new age will have a new style of politics, of education, of medicine, of architecture and city planning, of art, work, leisure, technology, family life, and religion. It is already being explored by men and women in all these fields, and it is already coming to birth through their combined endeavours.

But one question is central. What is man? What picture do we have of ourselves and our place in the universe? By what poetry and what myths do we seek to understand the mystery of ourselves? At each stage in human history the new vision of man seems to arise out of the new science and the new technology, but at the same time to be itself the flash-point when the new age breaks into consciousness, so that we can say, 'Aha! Now I understand what I am—now I am free to act in a new way.'

In AD 1300, in the middle of what we call the Middle Ages, Dante began to write his *Divine Comedy*, in which he describes his journey and the journey of Everyman through hell, purgatory and paradise. According to the cosmology of his day the earth is the centre of the universe, and God is enthroned beyond the turning spheres in the Empyrean, the highest heaven. In 1473 Copernicus was born. The Middle Ages were passing into the Renaissance, and Copernicus gathered together the new knowledge of his generation and articulated a new picture of the universe in which the earth was no longer the centre. The profound significance of his theory was that there is no physical centre – the centre is anywhere and everywhere, which means that Everyman is potentially the centre of the universe. And what of God? He is no longer in some place outside the universe, for there is no such place, but he, the transcendent God, is enthroned in the heart of Everyman. This insight is not contrary to Dante's vision – he had expressed it in the last verse of the last canto of his great poem when the love of the transcendent God takes possession of his heart. But there is now a *reorientation*, and with this new perspective a new age is born. There is literally a renaissance, a being born again. Everything is transformed. There develops a new style of politics, art, religion – a new style of life.

If you stand in the nave of St George's Chapel, Windsor, you can see it unfolding before your eyes. The building of the chapel is contemporary with the life of Copernicus. It began in 1475, and the slender perpendicular columns, the ultimate expression of Gothic architecture and of the Middle Ages, soar upwards towards God. Over the arches is carved in stone a choir of angels singing God's glory. But the roof of the nave was not finished till 1509. As you look up you notice that the masons are no longer expressing the glory of God, but the new-found glory of man. The ceiling is richly carved with the arms of King Henry VII and members of his court. The roof of the chapel was finally completed in 1528, when Henry VIII caused the most magnificent carving to be executed in that very central point of the ceiling where in an Orthodox church would be a representation of Christ the ruler of the universe surrounded by his twelve apostles. King Henry placed in this central position his own arms, surrounded by the arms of the Knights of the Garter. It is not surprising that four years later he broke with the Pope, and set in motion the

Reformation in England, with all its consequences for good and ill.

A renaissance – a new birth – a reformation – a break with hierarchical superiors – the discovery of the independence of the individual. Five hundred years later we are in the birth pangs of another new age, and the central question is again, 'What is man?', or for each of us 'Who am I?'

By what myths did the men of the Middle Ages seek to understand the mystery of themselves? It is important to ask and answer that question, because a myth is a story which has a universal significance, and yields up a deeper meaning at every stage of human history. It is a story which nobody has invented, but which has arisen out of the depths of human experience. The story of Adam and Eve in the garden of Eden is such a myth, enfolding within itself a mysterious truth. Every child can understand it but no wise man has ever yet plumbed its depths. It speaks with new power at every stage of our individual lives, and at every period of man's development. This story of Adam and Eve expresses the basic theme of which other myths are variations. Man defies the gods, breaks a taboo, and comes to a knowledge of good and evil, with consequences which are costly but beneficial, terrible but enhancing. Adam and Eve lose their innocence and are cast out of the garden, but they have grown in self-awareness. In the Greek version, Prometheus is punished by being chained to a rock while a vulture continually gnaws at his liver, but he has discovered fire for the human race.

One of the myths of the Middle Ages which guided men towards the Renaissance was the story of the search for the Holy Grail. Perhaps if we could hear it again and penetrate deeper into the mystery which it both hides and reveals, it could guide us towards the new age.

The story is based on the legend of King Arthur and the Knights of the Round Table, who probably lived as historical personages around the year AD 500, at a time when the Roman Empire had collapsed, and Roman civilization was disappearing. Britain was being invaded from the East by Saxons, and the old Roman-Christian culture was being forced back westward into Cornwall and Wales. At this critical moment King Arthur gathered around him the Knights of the Round Table, and it is here that history passes into legend. The Knights were to be the companions of the king, and the round table signified their unity. They were to preserve the values of Christendom — strong men riding out to protect the weak, to defend them and set them free from the forces of evil.

At the heart of the legend lies the search for the Holy Grail, and here we have to jump five hundred years to about the year AD 1000, when the story begins to emerge and to be written down in its various versions. The Holy Grail was, according to some, the cup which Christ used at the last supper. In this cup he gave his friends the wine, the symbol of his blood, as his living presence which would be with them as they gathered round a table and remembered him. According to another version, the Grail was the cup held to the side of Christ as he hung on the cross, into which flowed his blood when the centurion pierced his side with a spear. In either case, the Grail symbolized Christ's life and presence, and this cup was said to have been brought to England by Joseph of Arimathea, and to be hidden in an enchanted castle. King Arthur's knights were searching for it, searching for the presence of Christ at the centre of the round table and in the heart of each individual companion as he rode out to do battle with the forces of evil.

This story captured the imagination of Europe during the eleventh, twelfth and thirteenth centuries. We read the story of an abbot preaching to his monks who were nodding off into sleep, until suddenly he said, 'And now I will tell you the story of the search for the Holy Grail', when immediately they woke up and listened eagerly. These were the centuries of the crusades, when knights were riding off to smite the wicked Saracen, and to recover the Holy Places. But it was beginning to dawn within their consciousness that the battle between good and evil was not quite so simple as that. It was not altogether true to say,

'Christendom is good, and the heathen are bad.' It was not enough to ride out as knights in shining armour and to attack the evil in somebody else. Good and evil were mysteriously linked in a man's own personality, and if he was to ride off to do battle with evil, perhaps he would have to adventure deep within his own heart.

In what is probably the original version of the story, the Holy Grail was found by Perceval. He began life as a shy clumsy boy, whose father had been killed, and who lived alone with his mother in the heart of a tangled forest. His first adventure was to break away from his mother, and to find his way to the court of King Arthur, where he was accepted and put under training to become a Knight of the Round Table. His tutor instructed him in the lore of chivalry, and above all laid upon him the duty of obedience – a Knight of the Round Table should not ask questions.

When his training was complete, Sir Perceval rode out on his adventures, and very soon discovered the enchanted castle of the Holy Grail. He entered the castle, and saw both the Grail itself, the symbol of the presence of Christ, and also the bleeding spear. This was the spear with which the centurion had pierced Christ's side, and which was the symbol of the interlocking of good and evil – for the very same cruel blow which tore open his flesh had been the means whereby his life-blood flowed and became available to us. Perceval met the guardian of the Holy Grail, King Fisherman, who was grievously wounded in the groin, and could not recover until his heir should appear. In him there begins to appear the cost of winning the Grail – that a man may have to be wounded in the most intimate part of himself, and even in some sense to become impotent, before he can be trusted to become its guardian. Perceval sees also, in the background, a very frail old king, who is being fed from the Holy Grail.

Confronted by these things, Perceval does not ask any questions. He acts in obedience to the code of behaviour he has been taught. But this is his sin, and because he asks no questions he has to ride away again and search for another ten years, during which time King Arthur's court languishes, a blight lies over the whole country and the rivers run dry. Before he leaves the castle, Perceval is given a sword with which to fight, which is so wrought that it will never break, except in one circumstance known only to the sword-smith.

For ten years he searches and fights. He slays giants and dragons, he breaks spells, he ventures into dreadful dangers and darkness – and all these adventures symbolize the peril-ous journey which every man can make into the interior of himself and which some heroes in story and in real life have actually made. In the end he comes face to face with the knight Orguelleus (whose name means false pride, *orgueil*) and in a terrible battle his sword breaks. He comes face to face with the truth that the best thing within him is also the worst, that his pride in being a Knight of the Round Table is his fatal weakness, that in himself good and evil are interlocked.

So, broken and humbled, he comes back to the castle of the Holy Grail. Now again he sees the cup, and the bleed-ing spear, he sees King Fisherman and the old frail king being fed from the Grail, and now he asks the crucial question by which the world is redeemed. He asks, 'Whom does the Grail serve?'

The Grail, for which the Knights of the Round Table have been searching, is the symbol of the presence of Christ in the soul of man. Hitherto it has been held captive in an enchanted castle. It has been a pious and a romantic ideal. What Perceval has dared to do is to bring it into con-sciousness. The presence of Christ in his own heart is a reality which can now be faced and questioned. What is more, it is a reality which must be shared. 'Whom does the Grail serve?' It is not just a static presence to be adored and enjoyed, it is a spirit which must flow through a man for the service and the healing of others.

When Perceval asks that question for the first time he 'achieves the Grail', and a particular healing immediately takes place. It is the healing between the generations. The answer to the question, 'Whom does the Grail serve?' is 'Your grandfather – the old king is your grandfather, and King Fisherman is your uncle, your mother's brother. You have found and recognized your ancestors, and you have seen and understood that they in their generation were fed from the Holy Grail and were its guardians. Your ancestors have recognized you, their heir, and now King Fisherman's wound can be healed, and the old king can depart in peace. For now you, at terrible cost and humbled in your pride, are ready to feed from the Holy Grail and become its guardian. They can entrust it to you, knowing that you will be true to the insights of your generation as they were to theirs, and that you will hand it on faithfully to the future.' Now the new age can be born – the age when man has brought up into consciousness the three truths which together form the basis of his new self-awareness – that *good and evil interlock*, that the end of our searching is the *presence of Christ*, and that *all things are one*.

For through the story there runs this mysterious thread, that all things are interrelated. The search for the Grail is the concern not only of Perceval but of the whole country, both of man and of nature. When he finds it the rivers flow again. The generation gap is closed – past, present and future are united as they feed upon and serve the presence. As for Perceval, in finding the Grail he finds himself, and at the same time his human relations, and the divine life.

2. *The Catastrophe*

We must now return to the crisis of our own time. Before we consider the claim that the human race is approaching an evolutionary leap forward in the realm of the spirit, we must focus upon the other aspect of the crisis, about which there can be little doubt, that we are being swept towards catastrophe.

The factors leading towards catastrophe are now generally recognized, and they are rehearsed almost daily on television and in the press – overpopulation, famine, pollution, the danger of nuclear war, the gap between rich and poor, violence, the growth of great cities. As we look at this list we see that everywhere good and evil are interlocked in a tragic ambiguity.

Overpopulation is the consequence of an advance in medicine which has raised our expectation of life, so that for the first time men and women may reasonably hope to enjoy maturity and ripen into old age – but as a result we are threatened with starvation, and with neurotic breakdown as we crowd closer together without the privacy and the living space which we need to preserve our sanity.

Pollution is a result of the industrial revolution, and more recently of the scientific revolution which has set us free from age-long dangers and drudgery. DDT, for example, has gone a long way towards eliminating the Anopheles mosquito, and setting free millions of human beings from the debilitating effects of malaria – but at the same time it remains as an unabsorbed poison endangering the health of future generations. We enjoy a standard of material comfort which in the past would have been the envy of emperors – but at the cost of poisoning our soil, air and water, of exhausting our natural resources, and possibly of polluting our planet to the point of no return.

The nuclear age brings with it the possibilities both of destruction and of healing. The cobalt bomb could devastate a whole city region, but the cobalt ray, controlled and directed with precision on to a lymph gland or a bone tumour, may cure a patient of cancer.

The gap between rich and poor, the outbreak of violence and the growth of great cities, form a complex where this ambiguity of interlocking good and evil is most tragically focused. The modern city is at the same time the place of hope and despair. Here young men and women may grow up with a fantastic range of opportunities and choices which were never open to their ancestors. They can develop their talents through all sorts of specialized education, enjoy a variety of recreation, choose a job from a wide range of options – and if they feel so inclined change career several times in a lifetime, giving expression to latent aspects of their personality. They have available different types of housing to suit different styles of family life, and a wide choice of friends to be drawn from a cosmopolitan society. All this in contrast to their ancestors, who had no option but to spend their whole lifetime in the same tribal group or village, fighting off starvation.

But there is another side to this picture. I saw it one day focused in the person of an Australian Aborigine crossing a city street. Here was a man suddenly uprooted from a culture which was 30,000 years old, and projected into an anonymous concrete city and a maelstrom of moving traffic. He was detribalized and bewildered – and as I looked at him I saw that he represented us all, for all of us are now urban dwellers, and all of us are very recently detribalized, and bewildered by sudden change.

This becomes clear if we see ourselves in the perspective of the two million years or so that man has existed on this earth. It should be possible to illustrate it with a graph, in which the horizontal line represents time and the vertical line change.

We would get a picture something like that on page 22,

though in fact the page is too narrow, so that we can show only the last six thousand years, at a scale of 1 inch/1,000 years. If man has existed for two million years, then to show a true picture we should have to extend the time line off the page for fifty-five yards. During the time represented by those fifty-five yards, the change curve would hardly rise to an extent we could measure. Man

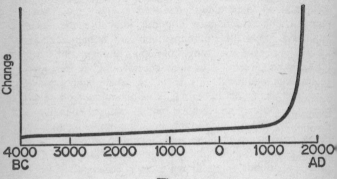

continued to live in small tribal groups, to move from place to place on his feet, to see as far as the horizon, to hear a voice shouting across a valley. Then about 4,000 BC, only 6,000 years ago at the point where our graph begins, the first little cities appeared in China and Mesopotamia, in Egypt and in Crete. Only two hundred years ago the industrial revolution brought the agricultural labourers crowding into the great modern cities to work in factories. Only thirty years ago we entered the nuclear age, the computer age, the television age. Now we can move faster than sound, and 'see' cosmonauts walking on the moon and 'hear' stars an unimaginable number of light years away on the edge of the universe. This scientific revolution affects us not only on the grand scale, but also in the intimate details of our personal lives – now we can have sexual intercourse without begetting children – and the upward curve of the 'change' line continues so dramatically that it is approaching the vertical. Already the sum of scientific knowledge is doubling in four years, and a piece of research may be out of date before it can be used or even published.

Against this background, what has happened to man? For two million years he adapted to his tribal way of life and to his natural environment. Without romanticizing this primitive life, which in many respects was 'nasty, brutish and short', we can at least recognize that he had the advantage of belonging to a human network, to which he was responsible and accountable. The Australian Aborigine still knows, apparently by some telepathic sense which we have lost, where the other members of his tribe are, and when one of them has died. He is in touch not only with the living members of his tribe, but also with his ancestors, and through them with the Dreamtime, with the myths of his origin and with the spirits of his tribe and of nature. He is integrated with his environment, being able to survive in a waterless desert, and to make use of every bone and stone and fibre, even the hairs of his own head, not only to make tools and utensils, but also to fashion works of art and symbols of religious worship. For him the past, the present and the future, nature, man and God, form a single reality.

We begin to recognize three facets in the 'humanity' of primitive man, which had evolved over those two million unhurried years. They concern himself, his human relations, and the divine life.

First, he used his own initiative and developed his own skills. He made tools, and weapons for hunting, and was proud of them. He responded to circumstances – to the changing seasons, to the weather, and to the habits of the animals, birds and fish that he hunted for his food. He was able to respond also to the internal rhythms of his own body, lying down to sleep when he was tired and getting up again when he was refreshed. He could be spontaneous. He could be himself.

Secondly, he was responsible to his tribe, not only fighting for them, supported by them economically, and obeying their laws, customs and taboos, but linked with them at a far deeper subconscious level, so that he and they were psychologically open to each other – their emotions, thoughts, intuitions flowed in and out of each other.

Thirdly, he had a picture of what sort of a creature he was, and of what spirits protected him or threatened him. He knew where he came from and where he was going – out of what womb of earth goddess, what myth of creation, and towards what Sheol or Hades or Islands of the Blessed. He lived and moved and breathed within some framework of belief.

Today, urban man has suddenly and violently to adapt to an opposite style of life, which isolates him, and destroys this unity with himself, with others, and with the divine life.

First, he is dwarfed by the gigantic size of the modern conurbation. He feels that he no longer counts, that his home can be swept away by a planner who is designing a six-lane motorway, or that he can be declared redundant by a tycoon on the board of a multi-national corporation who lives on the other side of the world and does not know or care about his personal affairs. His job is monotonous, and gives him no scope for initiative. He is bound to the rhythm of the machine, and must work a set number of hours regardless of light and darkness, or his body's needs for rest, or the joys and agonies of his spirit. He cannot be spontaneous. He cannot grow to his own potential, or be his true self.

Secondly, he is no longer responsible to the community. He is lonely in the midst of the crowd. He feels that he doesn't belong anywhere and that nobody cares if he lives or dies. He is not needed, and not asked to participate in making decisions. His life is controlled by some anonymous 'them'. In such circumstances the only contribution he can make to society is to smash things up.

Thirdly, he doesn't know what he is, where he is coming

from or where he is going to. He has no coherent picture of man, or of what values he himself should pursue, or what framework holds together his society. He has no purpose and no faith, either in providence or in his fellow men or in himself. Most serious of all, he thinks to himself, 'Nobody has any faith in me', and when a man thinks that he disintegrates.

As he disintegrates, society disintegrates around him.

In the civilization of ancient Greece an ambassador was sacrosanct. He was the means of communication between city states, and was protected by the laws of men and of the gods. In one of Euripides' plays an ambassador is accidentally struck, and a terrible vengeance unfolds upon the perpetrator of this immoral blasphemy. But within the last decade it has become common practice to kidnap ambassadors and hold them to ransom. It has become common practice to beat up, rob and kill harmless men and women walking in the streets of a city – in parts of New York people dare not walk alone after dark, or open their windows to let in the fresh air for fear of setting off their burglar alarms. Bombs are exploded in public places to kill innocent victims. Planes are hijacked and the passengers held as hostages and murdered unless demands are met – or these same defenceless planes, as they go about their peaceful business, are blown up in mid-air with a total loss of life.

These things were almost unthinkable a generation ago. They offend against the most profound convictions and customs by which the human race has kept open the possibilities of social life, and of communication between its members.

But this outbreak of violence, seen from one point of view as terrorism, can be seen from another as the struggle for freedom and justice. In World War II I served for a time with the Greek Resistance. We were called terrorists by the Germans, and heroes by the British. Some of our most devoted supporters were monks, who let us use their monasteries for secret meetings, and kept weapons hidden in holes in the walls and floors. The British were particularly warm in their admiration of churchmen who were ready to stand up and fight for freedom against the oppressor. A few years later another Greek Resistance movement began operating in Cyprus, this time against the British, by whom they were now labelled terrorists. When a bishop's house was searched and a bomb was found hidden in his garden wall, there was an outcry of indignation against the hypocrisy of this spurious church leader whose actions were so contrary to the teaching of his master.

Again, we find that good and evil are interlocked. Even in the disintegration of society and the outbreak of violence there seems to be a creative and hopeful element. At the heart of student unrest is a vision of a better world, in which professors and students will be colleagues learning together, and the rat race for money and power will have given way to a concern that people develop their true selves, and be just and compassionate to one another. A recent film *State of Siege* shows the terrorists in a South American city who are operating against a police state. They have kidnapped a US citizen. As they interrogate him courteously, and risk their lives to get him to hospital for some necessary treatment, it emerges that he is an agent who has come to train the local police in ruthless methods of suppressing opposition to the régime, including the use of physical torture. Finally he admits to his interrogators that he sees them as the enemies of Christian civilization, who must be exterminated by any means however brutal. We are left asking the question, who are the terrorists, and who the defenders of civilization, as one age dies and another comes to birth?

Our present urban industrial way of life is dying. It is in fact self-destroying, being based on a view of egocentric man which sees him as a creature of insatiable needs. Some twenty years ago Peter Drucker formulated the Marketing Concept, by which for good and ill industry and commerce is now dominated. According to this concept, the purpose of industry is no longer to produce goods which are required by mankind with the minimum expenditure of money, material or manpower, but rather to create a market. It is based on the assumption that man has limitless latent needs, which can be converted into felt wants. He can be stimulated by advertising to feel such a want, while at the same time the product or service to meet that want is being designed, produced and marketed.[1]

On such a basis we should be in danger of creating hell on earth, because hell is precisely the place where the souls of egocentric men writhe eternally in the torment of insatiable desire. Fortunately this could never happen, because before long our natural resources would be exhausted, our cities uninhabitable, our civilization in ruins – and towards such a catastrophe we are now being swept.

But good and evil are as always interlocked. The catastrophe and the evolutionary leap, to which we now turn, may be seen as interrelated aspects of the same phenomena. Man is indeed a creature of insatiable desires, but they might lead him to heaven rather than to hell if he could come to understand himself in a new perspective, if he could experience himself no longer as an egocentric island but as part of a greater reality, if he could arrive at that flashpoint when a new age breaks into consciousness so that he can say, 'Aha! Now I understand what I am. Now I am free to desire differently.'

3. *The Evolutionary Leap*

Evolution appears to take place in a series of 'jumps'. Perhaps we are wrong to draw a sharp distinction between evolution and revolution, because evolution may in fact proceed by a series of revolutions – or what certainly feel like revolutions to those involved in them. For example, the neck of the giraffe did not grow longer because over thousands of years giraffes kept stretching their necks or reaching higher to eat leaves on the tops of the trees. But it may well have happened that in a period of severe drought most giraffes died, and only those survived who had longer necks. Out of the catastrophe had come an evolutionary 'jump'.

The biophysicist, John Platt, of Michigan University discusses these 'jumps' in a paper entitled 'Hierarchical Restructuring' (May 1970). He points out that they often appear to be spontaneous, and without assignable cause. The organism 'goes beyond what it knows how to do', and this happens in many fields at once. He goes on to draw an analogy with human history, and to quote the Renaissance and the industrial revolution as such moments of collective change, in personal attitudes, ways of work, and economic organization. Such changes, he says, have certain characteristics.

They are preceded by a period of 'dissonance'. That is to say, one bit of knowledge clashes with another – new data do not fit the old rules of thumb. At first these difficulties are dismissed as crack-pot arguments, but after a while they begin to confront and challenge the old system. For example, at the time of the Reformation the current theory of the Church about earth and heaven, hell and purgatory, was felt to be 'dissonant' from the new scientific and religious

understanding, so that to buy indulgencies t
stay in purgatory began to appear ridiculo
phemous. Today pollution or city ghettos, wh
are crowded together in squalor, do not fit c
knowledge of ecology, nor our emerging image o
as interdependent *homo sapiens*.

They are overall. The industrial revolution was not only
a revolution in commercial organization, but also in the
structure of cities, in personal and political attitudes, and in
the quality of life men lived. Similarly today we see not only
advances in automation, electronics and transport but also
new patterns emerging in schools and universities, politics
and personal relations.

They are sudden. They build up over a period, but when
the forces of change reach a certain intensity, the old order
is suddenly overwhelmed from without and within. The
new patterns reinforce each other, and form together a
better integrated system 'with a speed of understanding and
communications and economics that the old malfunctioning
system cannot match'. When change comes, it comes like
lightning.

They lead to simplification. Money, for example, replaces
barter. Such a simplification enables a more complex pattern
of social life.

*They are brought about by jumping from the present
sub-systems to a new super-system*, and bypassing the established system which is unable to change. Today, for example,
the established system of national sovereignty is an anachron-
ism which, as Arnold Toynbee has said, should have disappeared six hundred years ago with the discovery of gun-
powder. We still cling to it, but it is being bypassed by sub-
systems, such as the great multi-national business corporations, which are jumping over national boundaries into a
new super-system of international world order.

There seems to be a mass of evidence that the human race
is in the middle of such an evolutionary jump, and that
the greatest 'hierarchical restructuring' in our history is now
taking place. But instead of calling it a jump, I prefer to

all it a leap. I can be made to jump if somebody pricks me with a pin, or makes a bang in my ear. But I can only leap if I gather together the whole strength of my body and my will, and deliberately spring. The difference between the evolutionary jump that we have to make today, and those which our ancestors made before us, is that now we can, and indeed must, make deliberate choices and co-operate in guiding the direction of our own evolution.

One sign that we are passing through a period of 'dissonance' is the confusion we feel today about our institutions. Teachers are openly questioning whether schools are places where education happens, or whether they are prisons where children are confined and true education is inhibited. Doctors are openly questioning whether much disease is iatrogenic (that is to say, caused by doctors), and whether hospitals are places where a patient is helped to get well, or where he has to be fairly tough to survive. Politicians are finding their countries ungovernable through traditional parliamentary methods.

Another sign of dissonance is our confusion about our 'roles'. The question 'What is my role?' is being asked at every level of society. As the whole system of social life changes, we can no longer define our roles in terms of the system which is passing away, and many young people are frustrated because what they want to be and do is not adequately described by any of the career labels which they might tie round their necks.

What, then, is the nature of the evolutionary leap which we must now take? If we are to judge by the whole course and direction of evolution over hundreds of millions of years, then we can guess that a leap forward will be towards a higher state of complexity. The original cells in which life first emerged were themselves marvels of complexity. Life advanced through multicellular organisms, through seaweed, fish, amphibious reptiles, insects, flowers, trees, birds, animals – until it appears to have reached a climax in the brain of man, where a thousand million cells communicate and interrelate to produce the miracle of self-consciousness. The whole process has been one of an ever-increasing complexity.

Now complexity involves diversity being held together in some kind of unity. Let us take as an example of complexity an orchestra playing a Beethoven symphony. Before there can be an orchestra, there must first be a number of instrumentalists, playing stringed, woodwind, brass and percussion instruments. If it is to be a fine performance of the symphony, each player must achieve a high degree of skill – he must be something of an individualist, prepared to spend hours in improving his own personal technique, and ready to play a solo part where this is demanded of him. But at the same time all these highly individual artists must be willing to be integrated into an orchestra. They must listen sensitively to each other, and achieve a balance. And above all, if the performance is to be inspired, they must watch the conductor, and respond to his every gesture, and even more subtly to his mood and to his imaginative interpretation of the musical score.

Here we have the elements of complexity, which are:

  diversity

  interdependence

  response to a centre.

We can guess that the evolutionary leap we have now to make will be towards an enhancement of these elements both in ourselves and in the society of which we are a part.

Diversity demands that each person shall become an individual, and learn to stand alone. As we look again at the Aborigine crossing the city street in Australia, we see that this process of individuation must inevitably take place as mankind emerges out of the tribal system. The essence of the city is specialization – each person becomes a builder, a tailor, a grocer. As the city develops, our specializations become more particular, so that in London there is a tailor in Piccadilly selling only tropical clothing and a bookshop in the Charing Cross Road selling only Penguin paperbacks. As our scientific knowledge increases a doctor becomes a specialist not only in cancer, but in cancer of the breast. As our management techniques grow more sophisticated, a company has not only a personnel officer, but within the personnel department a whole team specializing in 'salary administration'.

This same process happens in the life of every child. He leaves his mother's womb, the umbilical cord is cut, and gradually during the first two years of his life he has to learn that he and his mother are separate individuals. Instinctively she plays with him the ancient game of 'peepbo'. She hides her face for a moment and then her laughing eyes appear again. 'I'm not here. I'm still here. You are separate from me, but I still love you and protect you.' She is teaching him the first lesson in life's most important development – the movement from dependence to independence.

But both for the city dweller and for the growing child there is a second lesson which must be learnt – the movement from independence to *interdependence*. The city is not simply the area where specialists live alongside each other, it is the place where they communicate and co-operate with each other. In so far as this fails to happen the city disintegrates. In the same way the child, having grown up and established his independence from his parents, has to become interdependent with his wife and his neighbours. If he fails to do this, he does not provide the stable background for bringing up the next generation, and again society disintegrates.

So after independence, interdependence: after diversity, integration. And finally, *response to a centre,* for interdependence and integration cannot be maintained unless there is somebody, or some principle, value, purpose or belief to which people are ready to subordinate themselves – as the players in an orchestra subordinate themselves to the conductor. In a primitive tribe this centre of authority may be a patriarch or matriarch, who in turn is the representative of a god or goddess. As civilization develops, men learn to become obedient to law – a law which they may revere as coming down from God himself as on Mount Sinai, or as having been imposed by a great lawgiver such as Solon of Athens, or a code of laws which they have imposed upon themselves through democratic processes. (I shall always be grateful to the policeman who said to me, 'We are only trying to help the public to keep the laws which they have imposed on themselves.')

The evolutionary leap which we have now to make is into a fuller expression of this threefold complexity, which demands that we become more aware of our true selves, more responsible towards each other, and more willing to co-operate with the creative centre of divine love. The word 'love' does not appear at this point as an unexpected intruder, for the word 'complexity' comes from the Latin *complector*, which means 'I embrace', and embracing is the expression of love. The direction and the goal of evolution, as it advances through increasing complexity into the self-consciousness of man, may in the end be summed up by what we all know to be our deepest need and our highest experience – love.

At this particular moment in our history the emphasis would seem to be on our need to grow from independence to interdependence. At every stage in the life of a child, and in the development of mankind, all the elements of complexity are present. Yet at certain stages there is a special emphasis on one or other of them, as pointing to the exploration which must now be made, the battle which must now be fought. It is commonly suggested that mankind is now coming of age, which is taken to mean, by those who use the phrase, that we are arriving at mature wisdom. But a boy or girl comes of age at eighteen, and this is not the time of mature wisdom but the end of adolescence. It is the stage when he or she is emerging from a rebellion against parental authority and preparing for marriage, and for making a responsible contribution to society. If the Renaissance can be understood as a period when we in Europe broke out of a hierarchical order into an age of individualism – if at least the emphasis of that collective change was from dependence to independence – then we might understand our own generation as a time when the emphasis must be on interdependence – we must stop behaving like irresponsible adolescent individualists.

But if we are to change our behaviour, we must come to a new understanding of ourselves. We must ask again the perennial question 'What is man?', and we must answer it in the light of the scientific knowledge of our own day. Then, if we are grasped by this new understanding, if we really believe it in our guts as well as with our heads, because it is consonant with other things we experience in ourselves and believe about the universe, if we come to that flash-point we described earlier when a whole culture begins to see itself in a new light, then we shall begin to want to behave differently, and to find happiness by becoming what we believe we really are.

The scientific insight which seems to be of the greatest significance for our generation is that all things are interdependent. This is not a flight of fancy but the sober truth. The science of ecology, which was unknown ten years ago to the general public, has suddenly burst into our consciousness, and has made us aware that everything is interrelated in the environment of our own planet. If we tamper with it, we upset a sensitive balance. But this interdependence is not confined to our planet, nor to the present moment of time. It includes all space and all time. Every flower depends for its growth on the sunlight which comes to it from outer space, and on the soil which has been fertilized over millions of years by rotting organisms, and when it dies it will itself rot and contribute to the richness of the soil and the growth of other plants for millions of years to come. 'Every event,' wrote C. H. Waddington, 'contains some reference to every other event in the universe. It is a knot in a four dimensional network of relations, like a junction point in a spider's web.'[1]

In the light of this scientific insight, there is emerging a picture of man which could guide us into the new age – man who is no longer adequately conceived as 'individual' man, or even as 'mankind' separate from the rest of the creation.

Here are four examples of this emerging picture. The first two express the insight of young people, and the second two of mature thinkers in their fifties.

(1) A group of young men and women met in April 1973 to discuss the question 'What is man?' As they talked, it became clear that they no longer thought of themselves primarily as a number of individuals. They no longer felt themselves to be islands. If I tried to draw myself diagramatically on the blackboard, I could not draw a circle, and then show other people as separate circles to right and left of me like this:

O   O   O

I would have to draw horizontal lines linking the circles. We are interdependent not only in physical ways, but also in some more mysterious, psychical way – we seem to flow in and out of each other, to share moods, or to polarize into complementary attitudes so that if one is optimistic another becomes pessimistic. And having linked myself horizontally to my neighbours, I still have not shown a true diagrammatic picture of myself. I have to draw vertical lines, showing that the past and the future also flow into me and out of me. The past, my ancestors, the whole history of man, the collective unconscious of all that he has ever thought and imagined, hoped and feared, my origins in nature and in a divine creative source, all these flow into me and inform me – I look backwards and inwards and uncover, understand, accept, respond. The future, my children, my purpose, the unfolding destiny of the human race, the ultimate vision of God, all these draw me – I look forwards and outwards and give myself to them. To represent myself more adequately the diagram has to look like this.

(2) A girl of fifteen, whose mother had recently died, got up at four in the morning in March 1974 and went for a long walk in the rain. About two hours later, as the dawn came, she was standing in a field, soaked and tired, but with a deep sense of communion with the whole of nature and with the unseen world. 'You may think I'm mad,' she said, 'but I just knew that the trees and the grass and the rain were in me, and that nature and me and everyone, including God, were all one.'

(3) Professor Raymond Panikkar spoke in April 1974 on the theme 'What is man?' at a conference which included representatives of the great traditional world faiths, Hindus, Buddhists, Sikhs, Jews, Christians and Moslems. He is himself a man of the new age, who does not fit into the categories of the old. He is neither of the West nor of the East, since one of his parents was Spanish and the other Indian. He spends a part of each year teaching at the University of Santa Barbara in affluent California, and another part living over a Hindu temple in Benares and sharing in the poverty of India. He has studied and written in the fields of philosophy, psychology, sociology and theology. A Catholic priest, he has written a book about the hidden Christ at the heart of Hinduism.

Raymond Panikkar spoke of the three periods through which man's self-consciousness has passed.

First, as primitive man, he experiences himself as *part of nature*. He lives in a close-knit relationship with his neighbours and his environment. He is not conscious of nature in the same way that he is not conscious of his own body.

Then he comes to understand himself as *above nature*. He is civilized, and lives in the city. He discovers the laws of the universe. He is a spectator, estranged from nature and estranged also from the gods and the divine forces which enliven nature. The threefold unity of God/man/nature is split. He has gained self-identity at the price of excommunicating himself from God and from nature, and now as he eliminates God and destroys nature he is left alone, a king without a kingdom.

Today he is discovering himself anew *in nature*. As an ecologist, he is becoming aware that nature is not infinitely patient, and cannot be endlessly exploited. Faced by ecological catastrophe, he is regaining an awareness of a lost unity, and bringing together again the three elements of God/man/ nature in a recovered innocence. This is not a return to the childlike innocence of the garden of Eden. It includes all that we have learnt in the last six thousand years of human history. It is not regaining a lost unity in the sense that we 'go back to nature', but rather regaining a consciousness that I am a part of the reality which I observe – that God/man/nature are distinct but not separable dimensions of this single reality. These dimensions are not to be confused, but neither can they be held apart.

All things interrelate. Your ego is not my ego, but if I love you, then you are not simply a second self which has enriched me. I love you *as* myself. You are not obliged to thank me for doing you a kindness, because in a true sense I have done the kindness to myself. Similarly God, who transcends me, is not only concerned about me out of moral goodness. I am part of him, as he of me. Again, nature is not an object of my exploitation, or even of my concern. It is part of me, and one aspect of becoming what I truly AM is to enter into the rhythm of the life of nature.

This way of looking at things is not theo-centric, anthropocentric, or cosmo-centric. It is wholistic. 'God is that being whose centre is everywhere, and whose circumference is nowhere', and I too, wherever I am, am potentially at this centre. All the differences and distinctions between God, man and nature have to be kept and underlined, but we no longer find ourselves excommunicated. We experience at-one-ment.

As Raymond Panikkar developed these ideas we recognized that each of our six religious traditions contained within itself insights which could develop and grow in the direction he was indicating. Finally he posed us a practical question which arises out of this understanding of man. Is the time now ripe to draw up a *charter of human responsibilities*? In the late 1940s after the horrors of World War II a little group drew up a *charter of human rights,* and there continues to be a need to protect the individual man and woman from the violation of their rights so that they may be free to grow and fulfil themselves. But during this one generation of accelerating change the emphasis has shifted. Now, if the human race is to survive, we have to become aware of and accept our responsibilities to nature, to each other, and to the Creator, and to discover the disciplines by which we may actually become responsible people who are able to do what we know we ought to do.

The fourth witness whom I shall call to testify to the emergent understanding of man is Dr Fred Blum. Speaking in May 1974 to a group of clergy from the Anglican and Free Churches, he carried forward the discussion from the point where Raymond Panikkar had left off, though the two men have never met, and were speaking to different audiences and apparently on different themes. He described the development of the 'true self' by which man can come to know in himself the reality of God/man/nature. It is by responding spontaneously and joyfully to this consciousness and this reality that he can become a 'responsible' citizen of the new age.

Fred Blum, like Raymond Panikkar, is a man of the new age. By birth a Jew and by conviction a Christian, he has studied in the fields of sociology, psychology and theology. He has taken part in experiments in community work in India, and in worker participation in Britain, and has written about new patterns of relationships between people at work in an industrial company. He has trained and practised as an analytical psychologist, always with the object of setting free in his patient the 'true self' which is centred in the divine love. He has studied meditation. He is so much a man of the new age that he has founded – or rather allowed to come into being and to form itself – the New Era Centre, an international group of people who, while continuing to work in the old structure, are exploring the possibilities of living in the new consciousness.

The pattern of the development of the true self is found in the words of Jesus. 'If anyone wishes to be a follower of mine, he must leave self behind; day after day he must take up his cross, and come with me. Whoever cares for his own safety is lost; but if a man will let himself be lost for my sake, that man is safe. What will a man gain by winning the whole world, at the cost of his true self?'[2] In this passage we see a distinction between the self (the ego) which must be lost, and the true self which must be found.

Before a man can lose his ego, he has first to establish it. Each baby is born with a unique plan to guide its development towards selfhood, but at first it is identified with the mother from whose womb it comes. It must separate from this mother, and learn to say 'I'. At the same time the child must be protected by a love which does not possess, but sets it free to express with spontaneity the uniqueness of its own personality. So the ego is formed, and in a healthy development is permeated by forces from the true self. A gradual shift takes place from ego to true self, and from ego-centredness to true self centredness.

This true self is three-dimensional. It involves a true relatedness

> to oneself
> to the other person
> to a deeper reality

and these three are always interrelated.

For example, if I trust myself I will be able to trust others, and at the same time to trust the deeper reality of which I and they are part. Or again, if I do not love others, it is no use pretending that I love God or myself. The three dimensions of the true self grow together.

The ego was more concerned with 'having' but the true self is more concerned with 'being'. As the identification with mother is broken the growing child learns a new relatedness, and the quality of the true self depends on the strength and comprehensiveness of this new integration with the rest of life. Am I related only to my immediate neighbours, or beyond them to the whole of mankind? Am I related to the hungry in India, to the man in prison, to the man whose soul is being ground to pieces in industry? Are they a part of and within the circle of my own personality? How am I related to nature? Do I merely observe it as an object? Or do I reverence it, and recognize my at-oneness with it? How am I related to ultimate reality? How far, if I am a Christian, is my daily life permeated and given form by the light of Christ, who is the centre of my true self?

As we get older, the significance of the true self becomes more apparent. Old age, for the ego-centred man, is a period of decline – in opportunities, in career advancement, in sexual powers. But for the true self centred man it brings opportunities for a deeper integration with life, for a higher awareness, for becoming more fully a member of the family of man, and for increase in spiritual power.

The essential movement is that of dying and becoming. This is the continual life process. Decline and death are on the one hand catastrophe, and on the other hand can be movements towards a deeper and higher life. This process is most fully expressed by the Christ who is nailed to the cross and says, 'Father, forgive them; they do not know what they are doing.'[8] He maintains the relatedness of the true self even to those who are inflicting death on him, and through that quality of dying is able to enter into a

!

new quality of living.

Fred Blum sums up the law of development of the true self as

> differentiation
> integration
> balance
> centroversion (i.e. turning to a centre).

This is the same pattern which we saw earlier, when we looked at an orchestra, to be the pattern of complexity – and so to be the way of evolution. We suggested, then, that it is more than the way of evolution – it is also the goal of evolution, for complexity is, in its ultimate expression, love, and love is both the way we are travelling and our journey's end. Now, this same pattern is presenting itself to us again in a third guise, as the law of the development of the true self and so of a new quality of human living. It would appear, therefore, that this pattern or rhythm describes not only the evolutionary leap which we have now to make, but the reality into which we are leaping, and the sort of people by whom the leap can be made. It is the way, the truth and the life – which is universal, but which comes to its fullest expression in Christ who can say, 'I am the way; I am the truth and I am life.'[4]

4. *The Christ*

Before we turn our attention to the Christ, we must stop for
a moment to look back over the argument and see where
it is leading us. As we look we become aware that a pattern
such as we have recognized at the end of the last chapter
permeates the whole material and texture. The elements of
this pattern are like threads woven together to make up a
carpet or tapestry. The idea which they are expressing is
essentially threefold.

The myth of the Holy Grail offers us three profound
insights. *Good and evil interlock within ourselves.* This is
symbolized by the bleeding spear which has pierced Christ's
flesh but at the same time has set free his blood to flow for
us, and also by Perceval's fight with his own pride, when
he recognizes that the best within him is also the worst.

All things are one. As Perceval searches within the darkness
of his own unconscious, society languishes, and nature lies
under a blight. As he finds the Grail, society is redeemed,
and the rivers begin to flow again. As he receives the new
consciousness, past/present/future are reconciled, and he
enters into a deeper relationship with himself/others/God.

*The end of our searching is the presence of the risen
Christ.* The Grail, and the blood that flowed into it from
the body of the Crucified, symbolize Christ's life that has
passed through death, and is now given to us.

The catastrophe towards which we are being swept
arises out of three failures in 'civilized' man: his *failure to be
himself* as he lives enslaved by his machines and imprisoned
in his conurbations; his *failure to be responsible* to nature
and to his neighbours as he pollutes the planet and com-
mits acts of violence; and his *failure in faith* – both to
have any faith, and to believe that anyone has faith in him.

The evolutionary leap has a rhythm comprising three movements, which are continually present and held in balance, and are together the way of evolution and of love: *differentiation, interdependence, response to a centre.*

The true self is three-dimensional, involving a true relatedness to myself, to the other person, to a deeper reality.

If we set out these triads in a table of parallel columns, it begins to appear that they are presenting us with a single pattern.

The Myth	The Catastrophe	The Leap	The True Self
Good and evil interlock in ourselves	Failure to be myself	Differentiation	True relatedness to myself
All things are one	Failure in responsibility	Interdependence	True relatedness to the other person
The presence of the risen Christ	Failure in faith	Response to a centre	True relatedness to a deeper reality

The vertical columns indicate the threefold nature of the pattern which can be seen in the insights of the myth, in the diagnosis of the catastrophe, in the ever-present rhythm of the evolutionary leap, and in the analysis of the true self. One section of a column does not exist, and cannot be understood, in isolation from the other two. For example, in the column headed 'The Catastrophe', failure in responsibility to other people involves both a failure to be myself and also a failure in faith. Or again, in the column headed 'The Myth', the good and evil which interlock within ourselves are not ultimately (as we shall see) in tragic opposition, but can become part of a greater unity through the presence of the risen Christ.

The horizontal lines each contain a cluster of ideas which point to one element in the pattern, or one movement in the rhythm. The first element is the recognition that good and evil interlock within me, so that I fail to achieve what I have it in me to be – in face of this awareness I embark on the painful adventure of differentiation, learning to stand alone and develop a true relatedness with myself. The second element is the recognition that all things are ultimately one, but that crazily I fail to live responsibly towards other parts of the whole, like a man failing to live responsibly towards parts of his own body – as I allow the consciousness of my interdependence to develop, I grow in a true relatedness to other people and to the world of nature. The third element is the recognition of the presence of the risen Christ, but at the same time of my failure to allow this awareness to grasp hold of me – as the light of this new consciousness dawns within me, I am reorientated around a new centre, and I discover a new relatedness to a deeper reality.

Again, one part of the horizontal line does not exist and cannot be understood in isolation from the other three. For example, in the middle line, the leap into interdependence (which it is now so necessary for twentieth-century man to take) cannot be accomplished without the flash-point of understanding that all things are ultimately one, and at the same time the recognition that we shall continue to fail to act responsibly unless we are transformed into our true selves.

So every point on the table contains a reference to every other point. 'It is a knot in a . . . network of relations, like a junction point on a spider's web.' Together they suggest a pattern which we do not yet see in its totality. They are like arrows pointing along a path and towards a mystery which is to be revealed when the time is ripe. They suggest both *what* the new age may look like, and *how* we may hope to enter it.

Now, as we turn to Jesus Christ, we discover that he is announcing the evolutionary leap into the new age. We recognize this same threefold pattern in the character of the age which he proclaims, in the nature of his own self-hood, and in the quality of the life which he sets free in others.

THE PROCLAMATION OF THE NEW AGE

The name Christ is generally thought today to be the surname

of Jesus. In fact it is the title accorded to him by his followers, a title which means king of the new age. Christ comes
from the Greek *chrism* (anointing with oil) and signifies the
one whom God has anointed to usher in his kingdom.

When Jesus began to teach, at about thirty years of age,
his message was this urgent proclamation: 'The time is ripe.
The new age, the kingdom of heaven, is upon you now.
Repent, and let a new consciousness dawn within you —
let there be a change of heart and mind and will, so that you
come to understand differently, feel differently, desire differently, choose differently.'[1]

The character of the new age is threefold. First, it is a
new self-awareness. It is the transformation of desire. 'The
kingdom of heaven is like treasure lying buried in a field
which, when a man finds, he hides, and for joy of it he
goes and sells everything he has and buys that field.'[2]

Secondly, it is a new relatedness to other people. 'I give
you a new commandment: love one another; as I have loved
you.'[3] This is the new commandment which brings in the
new age. It is a relationship of unconditional forgiveness.
The kingdom of heaven is like a king who forgives his
servant a gigantic debt, but when that servant refuses to
forgive his fellow servant a tiny debt, the king hands him
over to the torturers. So it must be with us. If we cannot
forgive, there is no place for us in the kingdom, but we
shall continue to be tortured on the rack of our own hatreds
and jealousies.[4]

Thirdly, it is a new relatedness to the divine reality. In
this kingdom, the king acts with total compassion, but also
with absolute authority, so that out of his own good pleasure
he may give an equal reward to everybody, whether they have
deserved it or not.

In one story after another, Jesus describes this reorientation of the whole of life. He is proclaiming an evolutionary
leap, and it has all the characteristics of other such leaps.

It is preceded by 'dissonance'. The behaviour of Jesus seems
to the authorities to be anarchic, and his ideas to be dangerous nonsense. He turns traditional concepts upside down

by declaring that 'the Sabbath was made for man not man for the Sabbath.'[5]

It is overall. It affects economic as well as personal and social life. Do not be anxious, he says, about food, drink, clothes. 'Set your mind on God's kingdom and his justice . . . and all the rest will come to you as well.'[6]

It is sudden. After a period of build-up, the old order will be suddenly overwhelmed. 'Like the lightning-flash that lights up the earth from end to end, will the Son of Man be when his day comes. But first he must endure much suffering and be repudiated by this generation.'[7]

It leads to simplification. Love God, love your neighbour as yourself. On these two commandments hang the whole edifice of Judaism, all the law and the prophets.[8] (Here is the pattern of the new age at its simplest – absolute complexity expressed in utter simplicity – God/the other/myself, held together by love.)

It is brought about by jumping from the present sub-system to the new super-system and bypassing the established system. The sub-system is a group or cell of twelve friends, who are to break bread and drink wine and through these symbolic actions recall the presence of their master. This cell will multiply, till a super-system is created which covers the whole world and brings all men into a new unity. Meanwhile, the Jewish Temple and the Roman Empire will have disappeared.

So Jesus proclaims the new age. At the same time he is what he proclaims.

THE THREEFOLD NATURE OF THE TRUE SELF

Himself. Jesus was the most self-centred of men. He said 'Follow me. Believe in me.' He spoke of himself as the Son of Man, that is to say the heir of mankind, in whom is brought to fruition the quality of life towards which mankind has been evolving. He spoke with 'authority, and not as the scribes',[9] out of his own inner knowledge, and not merely repeating what is set down in the book. He knew the interlocking of good and evil within himself – the story of his adult life begins with his baptism, when the Spirit descends on him and he hears a voice from heaven saying, ' "Thou art my Son, my Beloved; on thee my favour rests." And immediately the Spirit drove him out into the desert, and there he remained for forty days tempted by Satan. He was among the wild beasts; and the angels waited on him.'[10] There could be no more dramatic words to express the tension between good and evil. The same Spirit which makes him aware that he is the beloved son of the divine love, drives him into the desert to become aware of his fleshly appetites, his worldly desire for power, and his satanic lust for spiritual pre-eminence. The wild beasts and the angels are not merely around him. The beasts roar within his own soul, and the angels open within him new dimensions of truth and understanding.

He was self-centred: not ego-centred but true self centred. This made it necessary for him to go on the perilous inward journey of differentiation – to break with his mother; 'Woman, what have I to do with you?'[11] (a very violent phrase which signifies a radical separation) – to bring the secrets of his own heart up into the light of consciousness out of darkness, to discriminate and to know both good and evil. But it also made it necessary for him (for the three dimensions of the true self are always interrelated) to be the man for others, and to respond with the whole of himself to the divine centre. Where one of these dimensions is found without the others, or two are found without the third, there is not the true self, but a perversion of it.

Others. So in Jesus we find compassion. He knew what was in men, because he knew what was in himself, and he loved them as himself. He ate and drank with social outcasts, touched untouchable lepers, and entered into the fear and pain which is in the hearts of all men. In his two most famous and poignant stories he showed this compassion at work in characters who have lived down the centuries – the good Samaritan who had compassion on the wounded Jew lying by the roadside and recognized his neighbour across the racial barrier, and the father of the prodigal son who, as the boy came stumbling home in rags, saw him while he was still a long way off and had compassion, and ran and fell on his neck and kissed him.

In Jesus, as in the rest of us, prejudice had to be overcome and compassion had to grow till it embraced the whole human race. At first his instructions are 'Do not take the road to gentile lands . . . but go rather to the lost sheep of the house of Israel.'[12] Then, one day, he makes a journey into foreign parts and is confronted in the region of Tyre and Sidon by a gentile woman whose daughter is sick. When she asks for help he replies as a good Jew, 'It is not right to take the children's meat and give it to the dogs.' (To the Jews, the Gentiles were dogs.) The commentators try to get round this harsh answer, and say, 'Jesus was testing the woman's faith', or 'the word he uses for dog means little dog – he says it with a smile.' But if we take it exactly as it stands, we see Jesus growing as we have to grow – making a real choice – so that as the woman pleads with him, his own human compassion breaks through the racial barrier in answer to her need.[13]

This compassion also embraced nature. 'Not a sparrow falls to the ground,' he said, 'without your Father knowing it.'[14] Nature is a mirror in which he sees reflected the character of God – in the rain, God's mercy falling alike on the just and the unjust – in the flowers, his artistry clothing each one more beautifully than 'Solomon in all his splendour'.[15] There is nothing sentimental about this. The flowers are transient, here today, and tomorrow thrown into the stove. Good and evil are interlocked. The flowers are challenging us, in their tranquillity, not to be anxious about tomorrow, but to live in the present moment and to have faith.

The deeper reality. The third dimension of his self-hood is response to the divine centre. His relation to this centre is so intimate that he uses the word 'Abba', which is the most elemental and intimate word in any language. It is equivalent to the English Da-Da, to the French Pa-Pa, to the Greek Ba-Ba. In Aramaic it was 'Abba' – the first noise (together with Ma-Ma) which a child makes, and which continues throughout life to express the love and security of a home. This was the word which Jesus, uniquely, used to address the creator of the universe.

He taught his followers that the secret of happiness was to know your need of God. If this need which is latent in every man can become an urgently felt want then, he said, 'How happy you are – the kingdom of heaven is already yours.'[16] Here is the insatiable desire of man which leads him to heaven. It is not the insatiable desire of egocentric man which the Marketing Concept has taught us to stimulate, converting latent wants into felt needs for our financial profit. It is the insatiable desire of the true self for the divine love, which is given free to those who know they need it and who ask for it urgently. The Marketing Concept is itself converted and has become the way to heaven from the very gates of hell – as Bunyan saw in his *Pilgrim's Progress* that there was a way to hell from the very gates of heaven.

So as Jesus proclaims the new age, he lives it himself. At the same time he enables others to enter it.

SETTING FREE THE NEW LIFE IN OTHERS
The flash-point of change will be that moment when we come to a new understanding of what we truly are and when we know it in our guts as well as with our heads. The description of such a moment can be found in the story of Jesus and the Samaritan woman, as told in St John's gospel.[17] We must look in some detail at this story, and at the threefold pattern which unfolds within it.

One day, as he travels through Samaria, Jesus sits down to rest at Jacob's well. It is a deep well, at the bottom of which springs a fountain of water. Jesus is tired and thirsty. His disciples have gone into the town to buy food leaving him alone.

A Samaritan woman comes to draw water, and Jesus asks her for a drink. She is astonished, because according to the customs of her day a man should not be talking to a woman in such circumstances, nor a Jew to a Samaritan. Jesus is

breaking through these categories of male/female, Jew/
Samaritan, and is talking to her as one human being to
another. He is telling her about his own need, and asking
for her help.

At the same time, he is expressing his confidence in her.
She can give him water not only for his thirsty body but also
for his tired spirit. He sees in her what she truly is, because
he knows what he truly is. She is like Jacob's well. Out of
the depth of her humanity could spring a fountain of living
(flowing) water which is the divine Spirit.

How is this self-knowledge to come to her, so that the
water may flow? If only she can come to know her need for
his free gift of God! If only she can come to recognize in
Jesus what he truly is – the king of the new age, the Spirit
flowing through the flesh! Then she will ask; and as she asks,
giving expression to her urgent and conscious desire, he
can set free this living source within her, 'an inner spring of
water leaping up into the life of the new age'.

We must examine this last phrase with special care. Here
lies hidden the mystery which is the subject of this book.

What is this life of the new age? The Greek words are
zoë aionios: *zoë* means life, as in zo-ology, and *aionios* means
of the aeon, or age. Jewish writers of the time of Christ
were using this phrase in two senses. First, it could mean
'eternal life after death' – life that is no longer in time, and
is therefore timeless. Secondly, it could mean 'life of the age
to come' – life of a new age in time, which will be different
in quality from the life of this present age.

In St John's gospel, this second meaning has taken over
and absorbed the first meaning. What Jesus is offering to
the Samaritan woman is a new quality of life which belongs
to a new age in time. The 'life of the age to come' is something which men and women can enjoy now, in the present
moment. 'The age to come' is now. It is God's today. It
is the timeless present.

So we discover that the first meaning, though it has been
absorbed, has not been lost. In St John's gospel the life of
this new age is also timeless. It is also 'eternal life after

death'. But again this is to be understood in a new sense. The men and women who possess this new life have already passed beyond death, though they are still physically alive. Death was the 'life' they used to lead, the unenlightened life of the ego, lived in the perspective of egocentric man. Now they have passed from this so-called 'life', and have been raised up into a new life which is 'after death', and which is life indeed. Death has no more power over it. The physical body will still die, but this eternal life is proof against the death of the body.[18]

This is the life which Jesus can set free in the Samaritan woman, if she desires it and asks for it, and if she believes in him as he believes in her. If there is between them the interaction of faith (we will return to this idea in the next chapter), then the fountain of the divine Spirit will be set free to flow out of the depths of her humanity, and will become in her a spring of water leaping up into 'the life of the new age'.

This life of the new age will be three-dimensional. *It involves a true relatedness to herself.* She will come to know herself for what she truly is – a spring of the divine Spirit. *It involves a true relatedness to the other.* When she asks for the living water (and she has been told, 'If you ask, I will give it to you'), Jesus says, 'Go and fetch your husband and come back.' This new life has to be shared and it can only be experienced by people who are committed to each other in love. *It involves a true relatedness to a deeper reality.* Old forms of worship used by both Jews and Samaritans are passing away. 'The time approaches,' Jesus says to her, 'indeed it is already here, when those who are real worshippers will worship the Father in spirit and in truth. Such are the worshippers whom the Father is seeking.' To know the life of the new age, she must let herself be found by the divine Spirit, so that she may worship 'in spirit' – in the flow of the divine Spirit leaping out of the depths of her humanity, and in truth – in the realization of that three-dimensional reality which is her true self.

She cannot understand yet. Nor can we, yet. As he

talks with the woman by Jacob's well, Jesus is telling her and us something which for the moment we can try to grasp intellectually, but which later we shall know, quite literally, in our guts. He promises this on another occasion, when he cries out in the Temple, 'If anyone is thirsty, let him come to me and drink; he who believes on me, out of his *belly* shall flow rivers of living water.'[19] Out of his belly, out of the seat of his emotions – his fear, anger, hunger, sexuality – shall flow the living water of the divine Spirit. Then he will experience in his guts what formerly he knew with his head.

But not yet. Not till some ultimate victory of compassion has been won, which has caused within us the flash-point of self-awareness. This flash-point (which may happen violently and suddenly, or very gently as I come to recognize what I have known all along) will include the understanding that within myself good and evil interlock. The fear, anger, hunger, sexuality which have their seat in my belly are at one and the same time the source in me of irrational panic, violence, greed and lust, and of the divine Spirit which transforms them and flows out of them.[20] But for my self-awareness to penetrate into this depth is almost too painful to be borne. It will reveal to me how devious I am, how treacherous; and underneath this treachery it will reveal a cry for help, a cry to be loved, a cry of pain because I am not loved. I shall need help to bear so much light.

> Go, go go, said the bird: human kind
> Cannot bear very much reality.[21]

FORGIVENESS OF SIN

Jesus pierces through to these root causes of disease in order to set free the true self. This healing of the whole personality, through the setting free of the true self, is called 'forgiveness of sin'.

One day a paralysed man is brought to him on a stretcher, carried by four friends.[22] Jesus understands that the man is paralysed by some fear or resentment lying deep in his past. He says to him, 'Son, your sins are forgiven you.' Here is the first element in forgiveness, that the man should know himself to be understood and accepted with compassion. Then he may be able to understand and accept and have compassion on himself.

The second element in forgiveness is that he should experience his interdependence with others, in the give and take of love. In the case of the paralysed man this was not difficult, for he was literally being carried by the love of his friends. It was the faith of these four friends which had brought him to the point of healing, and it was when Jesus saw *their* faith that he spoke to *him* the words, 'Son, your sins are forgiven.' This fundamental principle of interdependence is expressed in the prayer which Jesus taught, 'Forgive us our debts (our shortcomings), as we forgive others their debts to us,' and in his own commentary on the prayer which presses the point home, 'For if you forgive men their stumblings, your heavenly Father will forgive yours. But if you do not forgive your fellow men, neither will your Father forgive your stumblings.'[23]

The third element in forgiveness is that he should respond in willing obedience to divine authority. 'Take up your stretcher and walk home,' said Jesus. In every one of his recorded healings there is such a command, to call out that response in which the true self will exercise its freedom. The command is to do the impossible thing – 'the organism must go beyond what it knows how to do.' If you are paralysed, get up and walk. If your hand is crippled, stretch it out. If you are disturbed in mind, go in peace. If you are entangled in riches, sell everything and give to the poor. If you are a leper, be clean. You will know the truth as you do it, the truth about yourself and about others, the truth of the Spirit flowing through the flesh.

The words 'sin' and 'forgiveness' are today almost totally misunderstood. Sin is a precise term which, as used in the Jewish and Christian scriptures, has three basic meanings:

to miss the target – to fail to be what I truly am

to break covenant with my neighbour – to fail in responsibility to others to rebel against God – to fail in my response to the divine centre.

The word 'sin', therefore, sums up the three symptoms of the sickness of modern urban man, by which we are being swept towards catastrophe.

Forgiveness is the act or process of transforming this state of affairs, so that a man is now on target, enters with others into the give and take of love, and responds willingly to the divine centre. He becomes his true self. The Greek word for forgiveness, *aphesis*, means also the relaxation of tension (as in a taut rope) and this seems to imply that forgiveness has something to do with releasing the tension of fear, and encouraging people to 'relax and be themselves'. This is why Jesus so often says to people, 'Have courage, your sin is forgiven, go in peace.'

But, though in the end forgiveness may be experienced as a relaxation of tension, as being surprised by joy, and as the astonished recognition that in spite of everything I am after all loved, the process of reaching this joy is very costly. There may be some lucky people who are naturally humble and grateful and who seem to be always relaxed and joyful – but on getting to know them better one usually discovers that they have carried a special load of suffering through their lives. For most of us, and probably for all of us, this joy is only reached through the process of death and resurrection.

So now we come to the heart of the matter. We say of Jesus Christ that he is the one who takes away the sin of the world. Is this true? Did he then, and does he still, in some mysterious way transform the sickness which is sweeping us towards catastrophe into the love which is the evolutionary leap into the new age? Is he the saviour of the world?

Only through death and resurrection. 'Whoever believes in me, out of his belly will flow rivers of living water.' But not yet. 'He was speaking of the Spirit which believers in him would receive later, for there was *not yet* Spirit,' says St John, 'because Jesus had *not yet* been glorified.'

5. *Death and Resurrection*

'The Christ event is focused in Jesus of Nazareth, but is not monopolized by him.'[1] Proclaiming the new age, being the channel of the Spirit, taking away sin – all this can be seen in the lives of outstanding men and women throughout history and indeed in the lives of ordinary people. It would be odd if it were not so. But we can see it focused in the life of Jesus of Nazareth.

This is equally true of his death and resurrection. We read of how, through suffering, he broke the power of evil, of how he rose again on the third day, and was seen by his friends, and entered into the lives of those who had faith in him. It all sounds like a fairy tale, until we discover that here is our own human experience focused and brought to fulfilment in the Son of Man. This is what happens, though less perfectly, through the deaths of ordinary men and women who are walking in his way – or who at least want to walk in it, seeking to be their true selves, to have compassion, and to respond to the divine love.

So before we try to understand how the death and resurrection of Jesus makes possible the evolutionary leap into the new age, let us look at an ordinary human death – a woman dying of cancer. Here I have to ask the reader to bear with me if I become personal, because my wife died in such a way, and it would be better (since the issue is so crucial) to speak directly of what I know than to wrap it up in abstractions.

Scilla would hate me to make her out as anything but a very ordinary mortal. She had polio at the age of twelve, and spent three years lying on her back in a hospital. This left her with a slight limp, and a weak right hand, and at the same time a certain gaiety and humanity that came through discovering a new dimension of life, that she need not be afraid to hand herself over and be dependent. She gave birth to four children, and as they grew up she developed as an artist in painting and sculpture, and then as a counsellor in marriage guidance and group work. She hoped that she might learn to help people in that largely unexplored area where psychological and spiritual insights meet. At least, then, I can claim for her that she was on the way, searching for that reality which was herself, others and God. But all her life she was afraid; she belittled herself; and she could not easily believe that she was loved and that the divine love could work through her.

Then, at the age of forty-eight, she was found to have cancer. Over the months, as her body disintegrated, she became aware of three things. First, that I AM. She could no longer be *doing* the things she loved to do – cooking, gardening, sculpturing, making a home, counselling, but she became conscious of a central core of *being*. Secondly, as her friends cared for her and prayed for her, she knew she was part of them and they part of her, and that she was literally carried by their love. Thirdly, she had reluctantly to admit that something was happening through her – when people visited her they went away with a new courage and freedom to live. We had to call this third thing *grace*, a word we had not much used before, but which expressed what was actually happening – that the free gift of the divine presence was flowing through her.

Together with these three aspects of consciousness – which can perhaps be described as I AM, THOU ART, HE IS – came their opposites. An increasing fear, a feeling of isolation, and a sense of the absence of God. She was approaching that mysterious point where good and evil are ultimately interlocked.

The same thing happened in our relation together as husband and wife. We had never been closer together. Other couples have told me of the same experience as they faced cancer together. Life had never been so rich, so deep. There was no need to talk or even to pray. It was enough to sit and hold hands, as an outward expression of the inner knowledge that our two centres were being held together by the ultimate centre. But at the same time we were split from each other. There was a profound sense in which each of us had to face this alone, and those 'marriage bonds' of which psychologists tell us, by which husbands and wives are held together through their complementary weaknesses and hang-ups – the need to possess and be possessed, to hurt and to be hurt – these became clearer to us in all their tragic ambiguity. We were aware of evil, and of mercy. Her room in the hospital was a battleground, and it was holy ground. After she had drawn her last breath, she opened her eyes and looked at me and began to smile and died. It was as Dante's last night of Beatrice in the radiant beauty of Paradise.

> . . . she, so distant fled,
> It seemed, did smile and look on me once more,
> Then to the eternal fountain turned her head.[2]

After her death there was that numbness which comes to everyone after the shock of bereavement. Then, after a couple of days, the conviction that I must remember her and help her on her way, but at the same time that I must not cling to her and hold her back. Over the following days and weeks I felt an increasing awareness of her presence, a deep communion of spirit with spirit in a new-found freedom. Now there were no marriage bonds, no compulsive inter-action, no pretences, but a new possibility of love and co-operation. It was as though death had done for us what we could only partly achieve in life. It had torn us apart at great cost, broken our dependence upon each other, made us independent, and opened up the possibility of interdependence. But I should not say death had done it – the divine love was doing it through death and through resurrection.

Now I was being grasped by a truth which formerly I was trying to grasp – a belief in the resurrection of the dead and the life of the age to come. This truth was not

dependent on extra-sensory perception, though many people
have told me how quite unhysterically and unexpectedly they
have seen again those whom they had loved and lost. A
number of coincidences occurred, which were utterly astonishing and convincing and brought messages of love – but
these are only convincing to the people to whom they happen,
and in any case they are only peripheral signs. The central
awareness was that in spite of all our sin (and I use the word
in its exact sense of our failure to be ourselves, to keep
covenant with each other, and to have faith) my true self
and her true self were held together by the divine love, as
the two halves of a cracked piece of wood are held together
by an unbreakable rivet of steel.

So from this ordinary human experience we turn back
to the focal point of Jesus of Nazareth.

The secret of how Jesus sets men free through death
and resurrection cannot be grasped and set down in words.
It is the experience of being grasped when words fail,
and all we can do is to point again to the story and expose
ourselves to the experience.

Three facets of the story seem to call out to our generation.

(a) *Jesus penetrated to the roots of human nature, and
knew good and evil.* St John describes in chapter 13 how, on
the evening before his death, sitting round the table with
his friends, he knew that the hour had come that he should
cross over from this world (cosmos) to the Father. The
hour had come for him, as the Son of Man, to make for
all men the evolutionary leap, and to cross over from the
world whose centre is our individual self-interest, to the
world whose centre is the Abba Father. St John describes his
self-awareness in three phrases, which reveal his relatedness
to himself, to others, and to God.

Himself. 'Knowing that the Father had entrusted everything into his hands.' He is conscious of himself not only
as the beloved Son, but also as the envoy plenipotentiary.
The Father believes in him and depends on him. Whatever

has now to be done, he must choose, and he must do it.

Others. 'Having loved his own who were in the cosmos, he loved them to the uttermost.' The word for love is *agape*, the divine love of which he was the agent. The words for 'to the uttermost', are *eis telos*, which mean if we translate them literally 'into the end, or goal'. By an act of unambiguous love, in which the divine love will be acting through his human love, he will carry his own out of the cosmos and into the new age.

God. 'Knowing that he had come out from God, and was going back to God.' He is the living water, springing from the source which is the divine love, and flowing back into the ocean of the divine love. He is the river of grace.

Here is the three-dimensional awareness which we have groped after and dared to call the true self consciousness. Focused and fulfilled in Jesus of Nazareth, it is revealed as the Christ consciousness.

But this awareness is no honey-sweet tranquillity. As he passed through death he experienced its negative aspects.

Himself. He knew fear in his own belly – that paralysing fear which he had exorcized in others – as he knelt in an agony while the sweat rolled off him, and prayed 'Thy will be done.' He knew the extremes of physical need as he hung on the cross pleading, 'I thirst', his muscles cramped, choking as his lungs filled with fluid.

Others. Already there was treachery at the heart of their company as he and his friends sat so intimately round the table. 'The devil had already put it into the heart of Judas son of Simon Iscariot to betray him.' As he faced this treachery, and allowed it, 'Jesus was shaken in his spirit' – not in his psyche, but in his spirit – the treachery reverberated through the whole range of his personality which included himself, others, and God. Later that night the whole company of his friends failed him. His three particular friends slept when he needed them to stay awake, all of them ran away when he was arrested, and the one whom he had chosen as leader showed a total misunderstanding of his way by first attacking with a sword, and then creeping into his trial in what was probably a brave rescue attempt, but which ended in a public denial: 'I do not know this man.' The High Priest accused him out of jealousy. The Governor allowed him to be condemned in order to save his own career. The Roman soldiers beat up this helpless and despicable native. The mob shouted for his death because he would not lead an armed rebellion. The religious leaders taunted him with failure and blasphemy as he was dying. All this he accepted. He felt its full force because by the very nature of *agape* he was part of them and they were part of him, and he said, 'Abba Father, forgive them, for they do not know what they are doing' – save them out of this illusion into true self-knowledge and compassion and faith.

God. He lost his awareness of the Abba Father, and out of the darkness he cried, 'My God, my God, why hast thou forsaken me?' This is the ultimate horror.

He came to the point where good and evil interlock.

(b) *At this point of weakness something happened which we can only express negatively.* 'Not that! Not that!', as we gaze into the cloud of unknowing. We may say

> Things fall apart, the centre cannot hold . . .
> The blood-dimmed tide is loosed, and everywhere
> The ceremony of innocence is drowned.[3]

No, not that! The centre held him.

'He descended into Hell.' No, not that! Hell ascended into him, from the dark depths of unconsciousness into the light, and was transformed.

'He rose again from the dead.' No, not that! Death itself was the way and the glory.

> And thou most kind and gentle death
> Waiting to hush our latest breath,
> Thou leadest home the child of God
> And Christ our Lord the way hath trod.[4]

Words have to be uttered, but only that they may fail and fall short. Dante knew this as he reached the end of his journey through Hell and Purgatory and Paradise, and turned from Beatrice who had brought him so far to gaze into the radiance of the divine light. It was not that the light blinded him – not that! He would have gone blind if he had looked away. He tried to understand – and then in a flash what he had longed for gave itself to him, all things were made one, and understanding was transformed into love.

> Thither my own wings would not carry me,
> But that a flash my understanding clove,
> Whence its desire came to it suddenly.
>
> High phantasy lost power and here broke off;
> Yet, as a wheel moves smoothly, free from jars,
> My will and my desire were turned by love,
> The love that moves the sun and the other stars.[5]

When we fail to express what happened we are not saying nothing. We are pointing to the ultimate truth which will not be grasped, but which is able to grasp us. That is the heart of the whole matter. *Being grasped by truth is called faith.* People talk about making a leap of faith, but no, not that! The leap of faith is not something I do, but something in which I can co-operate. It is the living water leaping out of my belly, but only when like Dante, and like the woman at Jacob's well, I have come to desire it and to will it.

(c) *After his death, an awareness of his presence.* As the first shock and numbness began to wear off Mary Magdalene was weeping by his tomb, and she heard her name spoken, and the firm command, 'Do not cling to me.'

How do we understand the appearances of the risen Christ? We read that at the moment when Jesus died, 'the veil of the Temple was rent in two from top to bottom.' That veil was the curtain which hung between the sanctuary or holy place where the altar stood, and the Holy of Holies in which was the mercy seat of God. It hung between the place where men offer sacrifices, and the place where the divine mercy dwells. Now, symbolically, the veil between God and man, between heaven and earth, is rent and communication is open between us. Does that mean that those who have faith and love can now see more clearly the divine presence within the physical world? Or does it mean that they are granted a more open clairvoyance and clairaudience into the life of heaven? Did Mary see the gardener, and Jesus in the gardener, or did she 'see Jesus'? The writers who describe what happened are emphasizing two aspects of these events — that it was to those who loved and believed in him that Jesus was present, but also that this presence was not a subjective experience. Faith and love revealed a presence which others did not see — but there is nothing extraordinary about that, because in any case people only see what they are capable of seeing. A biologist friend of mine, walking along the seashore, can see forms of life which I never knew existed.

But these are only peripheral signs, given to encourage us in our grief and bewilderment. The central experience is the risen presence, saying on Easter morning, 'Do not cling to me.' I am on the way. 'Go and tell my brothers that I am ascending towards my Father and your Father, my God and your God.' We must separate, but in our separation we shall not lose each other, because we shall be on the way together towards the love of the same Father, held together by the same divine centre.

Then, in the afternoon of the same day, as Cleopas and his friend were walking to Emmaus that same presence walked with them. Passages of scripture came alive, and suddenly blazed with the truth which they had been so slow to understand. 'It was necessary that the Christ should suffer, and so enter into his glory.' As they sat down to supper, and broke bread, and remembered him, there was a flash of recognition. Their eyes were opened. 'He was known to them in the breaking of bread.'

Again, in the evening, the students – for that is the meaning of the word 'disciples' – the students of this dead teacher were gathered behind locked doors, for they were afraid. Suddenly Jesus was standing among them, saying, 'Peace be with you', and showing them the wounds in his hands and side. These are his credentials – proving that he is the same person who suffered, and who said, 'Abba Father, forgive them', and who has won the right to stand now at the centre of each of them, at the point of treachery and denial, jealousy, self-seeking, cruelty and blindness, at the point of fear and guilt and remorse, and to say, 'Peace be with you.' Now their self-awareness is to be transformed into Christ consciousness. 'As the Father has sent me, so I send you.' Now, out of their bellies can flow the rivers of living water. He breathes on them and says, 'Receive the Holy Spirit.' Now you are my envoys plenipotentiary, and you carry in yourselves God's authority and my authority to forgive sin.

'Abide in me, and I will abide in you.' As you remember me, I shall be in you and with you. 'I shall be with you always, throughout every day until this age comes to its completion.'

The death and resurrection of Jesus is, in one sense, the evolutionary leap into the new age made by the Son of Man on behalf of mankind. In another sense, it makes possible the evolutionary leap for us, because it can be the flash-point which changes our understanding of what we are. This flash-point cannot be confined within any verbal formula or explanation. It is an experience to which we have to expose ourselves, and all we can do here is to draw attention once again to the three aspects of this new self-awareness towards which the risen Christ appears to be leading us.

Self-knowledge. In the light of the death and resurrection of Jesus we can have the courage not only to see what we are – the good and evil interlocked within us – but also to accept ourselves as we are, to let ourselves go, and to allow the divine Spirit to flow through us. This courage to see and to accept and to let go is given to us by an act of unambiguous love which carries us into the new age, and which sets each of us free from the ultimate fear that 'I am not loved.'

Interdependence. The death and the resurrection of Jesus lead us out of dependence, through independence, and towards interdependence. 'You are plunged into grief,' said Jesus the night before his death, 'because of what I have told you. Nevertheless I tell you the truth: it is for your good that I am leaving you. If I do not go, your Advocate (the Spirit of truth, or reality) will not come, whereas if I go, I will send him to you.'[6]

> Your dependence on me will be broken.
> You will stand on your own feet and become yourselves.
> Then, between us, there will be the interaction of faith.

When a teacher believes in his student (and this is one of the attributes of a great teacher), and the student also believes in his teacher (I know this to be true, for I was lucky enough to experience it thirty-five years ago with Professor R. G. Collingwood), then that student draws out of his teacher no longer what is written in books but the genius of the man himself. This genius lights up and quickens the mind of the student, and becomes in him not just more information, but a living truth which is now his own truth, and flows out of him for the rest of his life. This is the interaction of faith.

As we believe in the risen Christ who believes in us, we draw from him what he freely gives – his genius – the I AM which is himself. Now the student can begin to say with his master, 'I am the resurrection and I am life.' Now the promise of the Spirit can be implemented, because now Christ has been glorified. 'The water which I will give him will become in him a spring of water leaping up into *zoë aionios* – the life of the new age – life eternal, timeless, stronger than death.'

Response to the divine centre. After the death and resurrection of Jesus we live in a new perspective. There is a word which expresses this change of attitude, but it is a word which, like 'sin' and 'forgiveness', is generally misunderstood. It is *repentance*, which means a change of heart and mind and will, a coming to see things in a new light, a reorientation. It is a joyful and not a lugubrious word. As we have already seen, Jesus uses it in his original proclamation of the new age. 'The hour has come, God ruling as king confronts you now. Repent, and have faith in the good news.' This repentance will mean such a change of mind that we shall see the divine love confronting us now in every present moment, and such a change of heart that we shall desire and will this sovereign love above everything else. The risen Christ uses the word again as he sends out his followers to carry the good news to the whole human race. What they are to proclaim is 'repentance leading into the forgiveness of sins'.[7] Repentance is a way, a pattern of life to be lived anew every day. It is the way of death and resurrection, the way of change and of growth, the way of questioning what we thought we knew so that light will break into the darkness and we shall 'see more clearly, love more dearly, follow more nearly'. It is the way of responding to a living presence, the way of taking risks and making mistakes and being forgiven, the way which leads through suffering into joy. 'There will be greater joy in heaven,' said Jesus, 'over one sinner who repents than over ninety-nine righteous persons who do not need to repent.'[8]

Interlude

THE SPRING OF LOVE

THE IMAGES

(a) *Flowing Water.* 'If you walk along that path for twenty minutes,' said the Cretan shepherd, 'you will come to a spring where the water is exceptionally sweet.'

It was the last year of the war, and half a dozen of us in the 'Resistance' were crossing the lower slopes of the White Mountains in western Crete. These mountains rise over nine thousand feet out of the Mediterranean, and take their name from the snow which covers their summits the whole year round except for a few weeks in hottest summer. Inside the bowels of the White Mountains there are enormous reservoirs of water – deep silent lakes which are replenished each year by the melting snow, and which break out of the lower slopes in hundreds of dancing and bubbling springs. Each spring has its own character. One bursts out of the rock in a torrent, and thousands of years ago (for Crete has been civilized for six or seven thousand years) men first built a village round this generous and never-failing water supply. Another trickles out of a crevice high up in the mountains where the wild thyme grows, and the shepherds come in summer grazing their sheep and their goats. They have built a little wooden conduit, and hollowed out a pool, so that they can catch the water as it falls into their cupped hands, drink it, and splash it over their faces. Each spring has its own taste, and the Cretan in the high villages will be a connoisseur of water, as his fellow countryman, lower down on the seacoast where the vineyards grow, will be a connoisseur of wine.

In the first part of this book we have reaffirmed the religious insight that every man and woman is potentially a source out of which can flow a spring of divine love. Each spring has its own character and its own taste, but

it breaks out of some common and mysterious reservoir,
like those lakes in the bowels of the White Mountains
which are fed by the snow . . . snow falling from the clouds,
carried by the wind across the sea from who knows where?
So the spring of love flows from who knows where . . .
through evolution, out of each man's guts. Man is not in
the end lonely and ridiculous, tossed helplessly about by fear
and aggression, sex and hunger, guilt and shame, or by
economic and cultural forces beyond his control. He is free
– free to give, to suffer and to create – if only he can unblock
and set free the flow of that river from deep within him.
Then he can know, not from hearsay but out of his own
experience, that he is the uniquely beloved son of the
Creator of the universe – and so is each other person, and
that when they know themselves to be springing out of
that same silent and mysterious reservoir it is possible for
human beings to love one another, and natural for them to
seek communion with the centre of their own being and to
respond freshly every morning to the joy which lies at the
heart of all things.

The symbol of flowing water is most powerful and
evocative in answering the question 'What is man?' It is
a very ancient image used by religious writers to express the
idea of the life of God in man, and it is also a very modern
image used by some biologists, who talk of the living
stream, or the river flowing in a necessary direction, to
express the nature of evolution. On the level of the imagination they are using the same language. But the mysterious
reality which they are exploring is too intricate and manifold
to be described by any one image. 'Both science and
religion often expect the vital disclosure to come to a humble
student only through his study of a combination of models.'[1]

Such a combination of models clusters around the word
'spring'. It has four meanings, each of which illuminates the
other three, and which together might lead us toward the
disclosure which is 'vital' for our generation. The first is
flowing water. 'A flow of water rising or issuing naturally
out of the earth; a similar flow obtained by boring' (Shorter

Oxford English Dictionary).

(b) *The Leap*. A spring can also mean a jump, or leap.
As we have suggested in the first part of this book,
the human race is at the point of an evolutionary leap. The
old order is passing away. If you talk to any professional
man about his role in society, whether he is a doctor, a
teacher, a politician, a priest, an actor or a business man, he
will tell you that his role is changing. He is no longer quite
sure what he is supposed to be doing – how he fits into the
pattern of things. Similarly our natural boundaries, our
sexual ethics, our religious beliefs no longer make sense to
young people in terms of yesterday. It is a reorientation of
our whole way of life which is being demanded of us.

As the pace of change accelerates, it appears that we
are approaching certain technological limits. The air in
Tokyo, for example, is so polluted that special oxygen
posts have to be provided. The Russians and the Americans
possess weapons with a potentiality of 'over-kill', so that
they could destroy all life on the planet many times over –
and other nations are now joining the Nuclear Club. These
and other dangers seem to be pressing us towards a critical
moment, during this next generation, when we must discover
new ways of living together.

There is another scientific advance which lies close ahead,
and which makes the evolutionary leap no longer something
which may happen to us in spite of ourselves, but at least
in part our own option, with unimaginable consequences
for good or ill. It has already been shown to be possible
to take the nucleus from a cell of a developed tadpole and
to transplant it into the fertilized egg of a frog, with the
result that 'in a good percentage of cases this egg will
then grow into a fully fertile adult frog which is the
genetic duplicate of the animal from which the nucleus
was taken.' This may be 'the most revolutionary development in evolution in the last half-billion years'. It could
conceivably, for example, lead to the transplanting of a
thousand nuclei from the cells of a genius such as Einstein,

and the propagation of a thousand of his genetic duplicates. It emphasizes a new responsibility, now for the first time placed in the hands of man, to influence and direct by his own choice the course of evolution. Already to some extent he decides which animals and plants shall survive and how they shall mutate. 'Evolution by natural selection,' writes John Platt, 'is giving way to evolution by human selection.' We are on the 'uncertain threshold' of a new era. Interdependence and responsibility seem to be two of its necessary characteristics. 'If we can work with each other . . . we will find in our hands tremendous new powers and potentialities for the full development of the human spirit, and a wholly new ability to shape our future course . . . In terms of evolution it will be a quantum jump. I would like to call it, at last, the step to MAN.'[2]

(c) *Resilience.* 'Spring: an elastic contrivance or mechanical device which when compressed, bent, coiled, or otherwise forced out of its normal shape, possesses the property of returning to it; and chiefly for imparting motion, regulating movement, or for lessening or preventing concussion' (Shorter Oxford English Dictionary). Here is another model which can illuminate our self-understanding.

The mainspring of a clock provides the motive power which over the days and the years keeps the clock ticking. It is so finely adjusted, and exerts such a beautifully regulated pressure, that the clock will keep perfect time with the movements of the sun and stars. Gradually, as we grow and develop, we become aware that there is such a centre of authority within us, which lays claim upon us, and keeps us in a true relation to the rest of the universe. But it has this further character, that when we are 'compressed, bent, coiled or otherwise forced out of our normal shape' it gives us 'the property of returning to it'. This property of resilience is found to underlie some of the most remarkable human experience, and to throw further light on the interlocking of good and evil.

In the slums of Calcutta families live in apparent hopelessness, and in such degradation that their own human excreta, beyond the resources of the sanitary department to clear away, ooze out of their closets and block the paths between their houses. Yet in these slums may be seen crowds of laughing children playing games, and a visitor may be received into a home where three generations are living together with a dignity and mutual respect which we in the affluent West have lost.

In his book, *The First Circle*, Alexander Solzhenitsyn describes the life of political prisoners under the Stalin terror. They are tortured into confessing imaginary crimes. 'No need for a detailed study of how his torturers beat him, starved him, kept him without sleep, perhaps spread-eagled him on the floor and crushed his genitals with their boots . . . "The fact that he confessed proves his guilt" – the epitome of Stalinist justice!' Their wives are harried into divorcing them. Their prison sentences are suddenly and illogically doubled at the moment they should have been released. Yet it is these men who know freedom, and not their jailers or the whole regiment of officials from Stalin downwards who live in perpetual fear. ' "You can shout at your colonels and your generals as much as you like", says the prisoner Bobynin to the minister Abakumov, "because they've got plenty to lose . . . I've got nothing, see? Nothing! You can't touch my wife and child – they were killed by a bomb. My parents are dead. I own nothing in the world except a handkerchief. These denims and this underwear – which hasn't even got any buttons" – he bared his chest to show what he meant – "is government issue. You took my freedom away a long time ago and you can't give it back to me because you haven't got it yourself. I'm forty-two years old. You gave me twenty-five years. I've done hard labour, I know what it is to have a number instead of a name, to be handcuffed, to be guarded by dogs, to work in a punitive brigade – what more can you do to me?" ' The next day a group of prisoners in the special prison, a research establishment for highly qualified technicians, are celebrating the birthday of one of their number with a little alcohol purloined from the chemical laboratory and coloured with cocoa. ' "Think how fortunate we are to be sitting here round this table, able to exchange ideas without fear or concealment. We couldn't have done this when we were free, could we? . . . I will never forget the real human greatness that I have come to know only in prison . . . let's drink a toast to the friendship which thrives between prison walls." '[3]

This same resilience is to be found in the great crises of human history. When Jerusalem was captured by the Babylonians, in 589 BC, the king's sons were killed in his presence, and his eyes were then put out. He was sent with his people into slavery, and it was out of that context of darkness and humiliation that about fifty years later an insight dawned upon one of the Jewish exiles. He began to understand that a man might perhaps suffer for another man, a nation for another nation, and be to them a source of healing.

> He was . . . tormented and humbled by suffering;
> we despised him, we held him of no account . . .
> Yet on himself he bore our sufferings,
> our torments he endured . . .
> The chastisement he bore is health for us
> and by his scourging we are healed.[4]

We can all point to individual people who in our experience have shown this same resilience. A middle-aged woman with a weak heart whose husband is dying, nursing him for three months, sitting up with him night after night, and discovering within herself reservoirs of strength. A sailor in the war, whose ship has gone down, and when he lands his wife meets him with the news that their house has been bombed – they have lost all their belongings and they laugh together with a new sense of freedom and of belonging to each other. These are scenes from real life. They point to a spring within the spirit of man – a motive power – a resilience – a tension which is not a tension of his own ego, but is able to operate most powerfully when he 'goes beyond what he knows how to do', and can feel and know and respond to the tension of the spring within him.

It operates best when he is relaxed, and has learned to accept the good and evil in himself and to trust the rhythms of life. A trampoline on a children's playground is an 'elastic contrivance' which provides the boys and girls with an experience approaching ecstasy, as they are launched up into the sky, hang for a moment high above the world, and plummet down again on to that yielding surface which accepts them, gives, absorbs their downward momentum, and then, smoothly contracting, flings them up again in another superhuman leap.

(d) *Springtime.* A fourth meaning of the word spring is *springtime.* Springtime is the season when snow melts, ice thaws, and water begins to flow again. It is the time of warm air, full of scents, and of windows thrown open in musty rooms. It is the time of new generation and fast growth, of the migration of birds, of light, colour, music and festival.

Thomas Nashe, a young man writing in the springtime of the English Renaissance, described it in these words,

> Spring, the sweet spring, is the year's pleasant king;
> Then blooms each thing, then maids dance in a ring,
> Cold doth not sting, the pretty birds do sing:
> Cuckoo, jug-jug, pu-we, to-witta-woo!
>
> The fields breathe sweet, the daisies kiss our feet,
> Young lovers meet, old wives a-sunning sit;
> In every street these tunes our ears do greet:
> Cuckoo, jug-jug, pu-we, to-witta-woo!
> Spring, the sweet spring![5]

But spring is also a dangerous time. A time of avalanches, of glaciers melting too quickly, and of floods sweeping through villages. The pretty birds may sing 'Cuckoo, jug-jug, pu-we, to-witta-woo' but this is the season when the cuckoo lays its egg in another bird's nest, and the robin's breast becomes bright red, a danger signal to all other robins to keep clear of his territory. It is a time when the owl, with a nest of young, steps up his hunt for food and swoops more hungrily on the terrified mouse. Behind this springtime birdsong there is a riot of sex and aggression, of hunger and fear. The flowers may be growing fast in the garden, but so are the weeds. The housewife throws open her window to the warm spring air, but the sunlight shows her how dirty her panes are, and that the room needs spring-cleaning.

One has only to list some of the natural things which happen in springtime to recognize that they are also happening at this moment of history. Perhaps we should understand our own age better, and be more positive and hopeful about it, if we saw that within the catastrophe which is overwhelming us are the signs of an exuberant and dangerous springtime. It is certainly a time when amongst young people old conventions and dogmas are thawing, and the structures of society such as the class system in Britain, or the caste system in India, frozen for hundreds or even thousands of years, are melting and cracking. It is a time which opens up the hope of new freedom for the spirit of man – a new flow from the depths of himself – but also the danger, if the change is too sudden, of a flood of licence which overwhelms unprepared and innocent people. It is a time of sex, violence, hunger and fear. A time of migration from poverty and subsistence-farming to cities and affluent industrial countries, with all the prejudice and conflict and hope and disillusion which this provokes. A time when musty institutions are throwing open their windows and preparing for a spring-clean. A time of drugs and tranquillizers – but also of guitars and festival.

The monastery of Taizé, in central France, is a sign of our time. It is a community with a new look and a new outlook, where monks of different denominations and nationalities are living under a common discipline, dedicated to the search for unity. On Easter Day 1970, the Prior of

Taizé, Brother Roger, announced the 'joyful news' of a new springtime.

'The risen Christ comes to quicken a festival in the innermost heart of man. He is preparing a springtime of the Church: a Church devoid of means of power, ready to share with all, a place of visible communion for all humanity. He is going to give us enough imagination and courage to open up a path of reconciliation. He is going to prepare us to give our life so that man be no longer a victim of man.'

Together with the 'joyful news' the Prior announced 'The Council of Youth', which would be convened after a long period of preparation and listening, when the time was ripe. During 1970 about twenty thousand young people from sixty-five countries visited Taizé, camping for a week, celebrating the festival together. Each week the crowd was broken up into a host of small cells of seven, so as to make the exchange of ideas easier, and 'to offer a real possibility of living a fraternal relationship with others'. One such cell consisted of two Italians (boy and girl), an Argentinian monk, a Dutchman, a Belgian couple on honeymoon ('they were ever so nice and very spontaneous!'), and a Frenchman. The theme for discussion was the festival, to determine just what it is, and what conditions have to be fulfilled if all men are to have access to it. 'Those who took part well remember: awkward conversations in several different languages during endless meals; existential exchanges on faith, the meaning of life, spontaneous discussions going on late into the night; a bonfire in the crater (a theatre-in-the-round built by the campers out of rubble, planks and stones) with people singing in Italian; exchanges about experiences lived in shanty towns in Africa; the background noise of grasshoppers singing and guitars playing; day and night in the little village church, people praying.'

Many who came were not Christians, but all shared their experiences of festival, and the theme which kept recurring was *festival and liberation*. 'The festival sets free, leads towards others, cannot be without the struggle for justice.' 'Liberation from enslavement, liberation of energies, of all that is latent in us, all that is still underdeveloped.'

What is festival? 'For me, it is the struggle to make others free,' said a young worker from Brazil. 'For me, I am the festival,' said a black American girl. 'Everything I am vibrates, sings and dances, I love with everything I am.' 'For me,' said another, 'prayer is the festival because there I welcome someone who is greater than I am.' These three answers were expressed in many ways.

(i) Festival is struggle. 'Political commitment in the service of man . . . the fight against the ugly and the unjust . . . the discovery of collective responsibility that allows you to advance and overcome problems.'

(ii) Festival is the celebration of life. 'Becoming aware of my life and that of others . . . a strength coming from within . . . expressed by singing and dancing . . . to be capable of astonishment and wonder, of understanding the hidden sense of small things.'

(iii) Festival is prayer and communion. 'Prayer has become for me an integral part of a really common life . . . by faith I spent a moment of festival with my family. My mother was ill with cancer, and we prepared for her to die. All the family was together to live the event with God. Now that my mother is dead the festival carries on . . . Some people ask: Have I the right to live a festival, surrounded by so much suffering? The question is rather: Have I the right not to live it? Not if I believe in the resurrection. But the resurrection can only be lived where there is first the passion.'

One of the insights which came out of all this exchange was that those who lived in the rich northern hemisphere would have to listen to those from Asia, Africa, Latin America and to receive from them the sense of festival. 'We who live in the northern hemisphere have for the most part lost all access to deep values . . . In our societies all the stress is laid on productivity and efficiency. This preoccupation eliminates communication with others, joy, simplicity, mercy. So man has become poor.' A Latin American

girl asked those from North America and from Europe, 'Are
you ready to yield the privilege of being a rich people?
Are you convinced that every people needs to find its own
original ways towards liberation? Are you ready to become
poor? Poor in the sense of needing others, conscious of having
to receive from others, feeling deprived? Are you ready
to make that conversion, that revolution of mentality, that
will allow us to achieve our own revolutions?'

After spending a week together, the young people dis-
persed all over the world to form cells, to listen, to embark
on an inner adventure, and to undertake such actions as
should be demanded by their various circumstances, political,
social or personal, but 'always simple tasks, in the knowledge
that God does not ask us to accomplish wonders that are
beyond us'.

Each year they have come back, in increasing numbers,
and the monks of Taizé have chosen to pull down the
west wall of their church, and to erect a huge marquee to
enable their visitors to pray with them. Meanwhile Brother
Roger announced the first meeting of the Council of
Youth, which took place in August 1974.

'Spring, the sweet spring,' exclaimed Thomas Nashe.
'Young lovers meet . . .' But springtime is dangerous, as
anyone who embarks on the adventure of love is bound to
discover, and it is also transient. Nashe himself was dead
by the age of thirty-four and in his last poems he is using
those same jingling rhymes to express the sadness of
autumn.

> Short days, sharp days, long nights draw on apace . . .
> London doth mourn, Lambeth is quite forlorn;

and the bitterness of death,

> Fond are life's lustful joys,
> Death proves them all but toys,
> None from his darts can fly.
> I am sick, I must die.
>   Lord, have mercy on us![6]

As then for Nashe, so now for us. This is not a time for un-clouded optimism, but it is a time to be grasped by the realistic hope that comes to us from beyond despair. After the death of Jesus his followers remembered his promise that he would 'come again'. The password of the early church was 'our Lord comes' (*Marana tha*). Gradually they understood that this coming was not a physical event which they would see in the sky, but was a spiritual event which takes place 'whenever two or three are gathered together in my name'. Particularly it would be realized in times of danger. On earth nations will stand helpless, not knowing which way to turn from the roar and surge of the sea; men will faint with terror at the thought of all that is coming upon the world; for the celestial powers will be shaken. And then they will see the Son of Man coming on a cloud (the symbol of the presence of God) with great power and glory. When all this begins to happen, stand upright and hold your heads high, because your liberation is near.'[7] 'Nation will make war upon nation, kingdom upon kingdom; there will be earthquakes in many places; there will be famines. With these things the birth-pangs of the new age begin.'[8]

Now is such a moment in the rhythm of history.

Now is the Spring of Love.
The spirit flowing from the inner source
The leap into the new age
The pressure of the divine centre
The birth of joy out of death.

THE DANCE OF THE IMAGES

If we allow these images to play upon each other and to interact in a kind of dance, our perception begins to clarify the 'mysterious reality' which we have to be and do and obey.

It is a never failing spring of water, an absolutely free gift that quenches my thirst and answers to my deepest need. At the same time it is a motive power arising from my own

centre, an absolute claim upon me that I should fulfil
my own destiny.

It is, as it were, female and male, my mother and my
father, but now no longer as external guardians, but as an
authority rising out of the depths of my own spirit.

But it is also that which I most long for and fear, the
meeting with my lover, with my own true love, whose
coming surprises me by being so much more natural and
wonderful than anything I could have imagined. It is
'being found' by what I was searching for.

> Journeys end in lovers meeting,
> Every wise man's son doth know.[9]

It is courage – the courage of an artist who expresses new
ideas a generation ahead of his time, the courage to suffer,
the courage that arises out of fear and in the face of
danger.

> To be brave is to behave
> bravely when your heart is faint.
> So you can be really brave
> only when you really ain't.[10]

It is new life which arises out of death, and which can
only be had through dying and being born again. It is
a reckless self-abandonment, a kind of playtime and a
kind of music – a festival of gratitude, and a sense of
unity with all created things.

It is a leap forward in self-consciousness – coming to know
myself and other people in the same moment. For 'self-
consciousness', as we use the word in our common speech,
has this double meaning, both to be aware of myself, and
also to recognize with embarrassment that somebody else is
looking at me.

When in the myth of the garden of Eden, Adam and
Eve took the original leap into self-consciousness they did
so because they were tempted by the serpent – 'you shall

be as gods.' This is always the temptation that accompanies the leap – that we should say in the deep recesses of our minds which are hidden even from ourselves, 'I am going to silence my own secret fears that I am nobody, and enhance my self-esteem, and become a remarkable spiritual person who possesses occult powers and exerts moral influence over others.' These were the motives that were inevitably hidden in the human personality of Jesus, which is why 'for forty days (he) was led by the Spirit up and down the wilderness and tempted by the devil'[11] so that they might be uncovered and transformed and harnessed to his true purpose. This is why we too must be alert to all fantasies of the ego and delusions that we shall 'be as gods'.

The leap into self-consciousness will be the recognition that 'somebody is looking at me'. He is not like Big Brother keeping count of my faults, but with a smile of great love in his eyes he is saying to me, 'Try not to take yourself too seriously.' Then there is silence for half an hour, or perhaps for ten years, or for half a lifetime, after which he says, 'I will be in you your true self', and his voice is like the sound of rushing waters.

Part II

THE SPRINGTIME
OF THE CHURCH

6. *The Threefold Style*

Catastrophe? Evolutionary leap?

Are these alternatives? Can we hope to avoid the catastrophe, because in the nick of time the resilience of the human spirit will save us, and we shall adjust to the new necessity for interdependence?

Or shall we move through catastrophe to the evolutionary leap? Will it be only after appalling disaster that those who survive will come to their senses, and to a new humility, compassion, and response to the divine centre?

Or, the third possibility, will the catastrophe bring to an end this experiment which is self-conscious man? Will we become extinct as countless other species have done before us?

This question we cannot answer, and we need not waste time over it. Our business is not with the future but with the present moment. We live in a universe where everything is disintegrating, where according to the second law of thermodynamics the whole universe is continuously returning to chaos. Yet, at the same time it is a universe where the miracle of evolution takes place, where life rises to consciousness and through self-consciousness towards love. Our generation is a time when both these forces are to be felt reverberating with terrific power in human affairs. We see the old order falling apart. It is a time of anguish when we know ourselves to be falling apart, and when God will not intervene to save us. But at the same time we can see a new order is being born. We can begin to recognize within ourselves the form of a true self. It is as though we have to fall apart in order to be recreated in a new pattern – as though the ego has to crack and split open like a seed so that the new growth of the true self may break out from within – as though the divine love were saying to us with a new urgency, 'If anyone wishes to be a follower of mine, he must leave self behind. Whoever cares for his own safety is lost, but if a man will let himself be lost for my sake, that man is safe.'

What we have to do now is to let ourselves be lost, to stand still and see the pattern of the new age, and allow it to form itself and grow in our personal lives and in our relations with each other.

There are three signs of the new age which correspond to the three aspects of the crisis in which we find ourselves. We may call them contemplation, the group, and community work.

Contemplation. There is a growing hunger to know the divine love by personal experience. Young people everywhere are turning to contemplation at the same time as they turn away from the great traditional religions. They are not content to hear about God, they want to know him. They practise yoga. They follow gurus. They take drugs. They are caught up in Pentecostal experience, when the power of a spirit greater than their own lays hold upon them.

But it is not only the young who are seeking. Many middle-aged people are opting out of the rat race for money and power, and into a life where they will find more tranquillity and be better able to make the journey into themselves.

This hunger to know God is being accentuated and 'transformed from a latent need into a felt want' by that aspect of our contemporary crisis which we have called 'the failure in faith'. When a man no longer has a purpose or a goal or a hope, when he no longer believes in anything, and when he thinks to himself 'nobody believes in me', then he falls apart, and at that moment he experiences a desperate need. In the word 'contemplation' we have a signpost showing him the road that he can take and the direction in which he can travel to seek for the satisfaction of that desperate need for divine love.

The group. As cities sprawl out into conurbations and business companies expand into multi-national corporations, as things get bigger and people feel smaller, we are re-discovering the creative power of the group. One of the most powerful of the great multi-national corporations, IBM, has organized its employees so that each man finds himself in a small group under a supervisor, who will see him frequently, listen to him, be interested in his views and concerned about his career. In a London hospital, a group of doctors meet regularly with the sister and the nurses of their unit, so that through talking together they may grow towards a better understanding of one another as well as of their professional task – and at the same time they arrange the accommodation for the patients in such a way that they too may meet in small groups, and encourage each other by sharing their hopes and fears and their human compassion. In the great anonymous cities of the world, centres proliferate where one may experience the encounter group, the therapy group, the learning group – where people may come to know themselves as they interact with other people.

So, again, the aspect of our contemporary crisis which we have called the failure to be myself is urging us towards the rediscovery of the small group. It is 'rediscovery' in the sense that tribal man and village man have always lived and worked in the small group, and even urban man until recently depended upon his extended family of uncles, aunts, grandparents, cousins. But now, in our gigantic society where we are dwarfed, in our mobile society where we change our neighbours and our jobs so rapidly, we have to learn to do voluntarily what our ancestors did naturally, and in this process of learning we are discovering a new depth and freedom in human relations.

Community work. This is the style of living by which people are encouraged to help themselves. We can see it in South America in the work of Paulo Friere, who has developed a new style of education by which people are no longer trained to amass information which will make them servile and obedient supporters of the *status quo,* but to develop in themselves a new consciousness, through articulating their own political aspirations, and by acting out what they have articulated. In China, the emphasis of the cultural revolution is on self-reliance, and on a proper pride which prefers the products which their own workers have made in their own factories to technically superior goods which have been brought from abroad. Black consciousness is the awareness of the unique history and culture of the black people, and of the contribution which they can make to the world community. The rebirth of nationalism, whilst it can be a most sinister and disruptive influence, hideous and damaging in its effects, can at the same time foster the diversity which is necessary if we are to grow in complexity. Here good and evil are most dangerously and creatively interlocked.

This movement to draw people into active participation is evident in the arts. Theatre-in-the-round brings the actors amongst the audience so that the footlights no longer divide, but everybody in the theatre is creating the occasion together. Benjamin Britten's *Let's Make an Opera* uses the audience as the chorus, so that they have the great delight of rehearsing their parts in Act 1 when the opera is being constructed, and of singing them in Act 2 when the opera is being performed. Kinetic art invites the visitor to touch, taste and be involved. Folk music and street theatre invite him to join in and share.

In the first half of the twentieth century Britain developed the welfare state with its ideal of setting people free from degrading poverty and providing for every citizen a basic security. To implement the welfare services there grew up an army of social workers who served the community with great devotion, picking up the casualties of our society and trying to rehabilitate them. Now, after a generation has passed, we see again how good and evil are interlocked, and how the provision of welfare is accompanied by the danger of the loss of initiative. So during the last decade there begins to emerge a new style of social work, known as community work, by which a community is encouraged to express its own needs, and to develop from within itself the resources to meet them.

Once again, an aspect of our contemporary crisis, which in this case we have called the failure in responsibility, is giving birth to a new style of living. We are rediscovering what our ancestors did naturally, but now with skills and opportunities which enable us to set free as never before in human history the creative potentialities within us, and to share them with one another.

These three, contemplation, the group, community work, are not only reactions to the crisis of the present moment, they are at the same time the way in which the evolutionary leap expresses itself.

As we have seen, the leap is a leap into complexity, and complexity has three aspects.

That we learn to differentiate, to become independent and to grow through self-knowledge into the full capacity of the true self. The school in which we can learn to do this is the group, for in the group we grow in self-knowledge as we interact with others.

That we become interdependent. Complexity demands the integration and balance of all the independent parts, creating harmony in music, and love and justice in human affairs. The way to activate this interdependence – this love and justice – in our political and social life is through community work, by which men and women are set free to be responsible for each other.

That we respond to a centre. As the orchestra responds to the conductor, so the human group or community can only be held together in the beauty of complexity if it responds to a common authority or purpose. Our common purpose is complexity itself or love. The way of being grasped by the truth of love and responding in the life of love is exactly and precisely contemplation. We shall examine this in the next chapter.

It is significant that the young people at Taizé who began in 1970 to prepare for the 'springtime of the Church', and for the Council of Youth in 1974, should have embarked on this threefold way of the group, community work and contemplation. Here the life of the new age is being brought into consciousness and exposed.

This life, as we have claimed, was originally and very

recently (less than two thousand years ago) focused and expressed through Jesus of Nazareth, and the evolutionary leap into the new age was made by him and made possible for us by his death and resurrection. The life and the leap are not monopolized by him, but focused in him. That would lead us to expect that in the crisis of the present moment we should see signs of the new life everywhere – as indeed we do, in the new science of ecology, the new demands for justice, the new patterns of working together – and that we should see this new life focused and expressed in the Christian Church.

This is a time when we must abandon Christian imperialism, and the arrogance which has marred the history of the Christian Church. We must recognize that the ultimate truth is reflected in all great religions of the world, as well as in movements which reject religion as being the great hindrance to the advance of truth. We can only move forward into the new age together if all of us remain loyal to the insights we have been given, but are prepared to allow them to grow and develop and to pass through an experience of death and rebirth.

But having said that, it remains my conviction that the Christian Church holds within itself the inner secret of the evolutionary leap, and that it is a precision instrument, designed with an accuracy and timing and ingenuity beyond the dreams of human invention to make possible what the human race has now to do. Who could have dreamt up the idea of an international structure of small groups, alive with the death and resurrection of Christ, existing at the heart of every community, and being a ferment of love and justice? There is no other way in which the evolutionary leap could possibly be enabled. People cannot be dragooned or manipulated into love; they can only be attracted by example, and their free response won by compassion, and by sharing of weakness.

That is what the Christian Church is, and at the same time most tragically is not. Nowhere can we see the interlocking of good and evil more painfully and distinctly. Here is the compassion which sets men free, but at the same time the fear and the rigidity which makes a prison-house for the human spirit. In the Church is the fragrance of life and the stench of death.

But out of the frozen deathlike winter of the Church there is always breaking a new springtime, and when this springtime comes, it has always the same joyful and dangerous quality. In the thirteenth century it broke through the person of St Francis, the son of a rich draper in Assisi, who gave away his clothes to a beggar, and kissed a leper, and founded a brotherhood. His brotherhood had the threefold style, which appears in every springtime of the Church because it appeared in Christ himself. St Francis was the great contemplative, who saw God in everything, and knew that the sun and the moon, the wind, the rushing water, the flowers and fruits of the earth were his brothers and sisters. St Francis formed around himself a group of friars who would have everything in common, and explore together the life of simplicity and love. St Francis and his friars went and stood beside the outcasts of society, begging with the beggars, toiling in kitchens with scullions and on the land with serfs, not doing good to them, but encouraging them to understand and to realize their own dignity.

This same springtime, broke through George Fox as he founded the Society of Friends in the seventeenth century – the Quakers who quaked at the presence of the living God, and shared each other's concerns, and acted out the life of love and humble service amongst their fellow men. It broke again through John Wesley as he founded the Methodist society in the eighteenth century, with its sense of the holiness of God, with its cellular structure of house groups, and its passionate concern for social justice and political reform.

Now it is breaking again out of the churches, all over the world, like thousands of springs of flowing water leaping up into the life of the new age. Where its threefold character is held in balance, and where men and women are walking in the way of death and resurrection, there we can see reflected the truth and we can begin to taste the life of the new age.

7. Contemplation

Contemplation is the opposite of what it is popularly supposed to be. A young man who thought he had learned to contemplate once said to me, 'I make my mind blank, and then it is filled with honey-sweet thoughts.' This is in fact a description of psychosis, which is the flight away from reality and into fantasy. People imagine that the contemplative closes his eyes and shuts out the world, or that he retires into a cave or into a desert where he 'contemplates' his own navel. On the contrary, contemplation is an opening of the eyes, and a becoming aware of the world – becoming so deeply and accurately aware that through what he sees and through what happens around him, and indeed through his own navel – through the mysterious depths of himself and of his past with which his navel once physically connected him – the one who dares to contemplate finds himself confronted by the divine love.

Archbishop Bloom, of the Russian Orthodox Church, tells the story of a lady who came to him and said, 'I have been praying all my life, but I have never experienced God. What should I do?' He advised her to go home and tidy her room and sit still for twenty minutes. 'And whatever you do,' he warned her, 'don't pray.' So she went home and tidied her room and sat still, and now for the first time for a long time she discovered that she *had* time, time to look at her room and appreciate it, and notice all the colours and the architectural shapes. She heard the ticking of the clock. The silence grew profound, and she felt herself slipping into prayer, but she knew this was the one thing she was not allowed to do. So she got out her knitting, and what with the ticking of the clock and the clicking of her needles the silence grew even more profound, until at the heart of the silence *she became aware of a presence*.

That story opens the way into contemplation. We are learning today that it is not a specialist kind of prayer for hermits, as was thought in past generations, but that it is the natural way in which most of us do in fact become aware of the presence of God.

Contemplative prayer begins with having time, making a space for relaxation, so that our agitated minds can grow still and like the surface of a lake can begin to reflect the surrounding trees and mountains. We become aware of nature – of a flower, maybe, or of the falling rain. We become aware of people, of our neighbours, each with a unique personality and expressing a unique goodness and carrying a unique suffering. Our minds are not filled with honey-sweet thoughts, but with the reality in which good and evil, life and death, are interlocked. And as we become aware of the present moment, in all its height and depth and length and breadth, we become aware that through this present we are being approached by a presence. Most vividly do we experience this through ourselves, because I am that which is most immediately present to myself. Out of the reality of myself as I allow it to come into consciousness, out of my anxiety and creativity and joy and pain, out of this mishmash which is me, there is coming to meet me the divine love.

This is the encounter which is at the heart of contemplation. The story which describes it most poignantly is the parable of the prodigal son which we have already quoted – of the boy who left home and spent his father's money, and landed up in a foreign country feeding pigs, in a state of degradation, hunger and despair. Then he came to himself, and decided to go home. As he came stumbling back, 'while he was still a great way off, his father saw him, and had compassion, and ran and fell on his neck and kissed him.' This is the nature of the encounter, not that I am stumbling towards the Abba Father, but that the Abba Father is running towards me. It is not that I love God but that God loves me, not that I believe in God but that God believes in me. The discovery at the heart of contemplation is not that I am contemplating the divine love, but that the divine love is contemplating me. He sees me and understands and accepts me, he has compassion on me, he creates me afresh from moment to moment, and he protects me and is with me through death and into the life beyond.

Our contribution to this encounter is to let it happen, to remove obstacles and clear the way. It is something like drawing back your bedroom curtains on a summer morning, and letting the light come into your room. You do not have to search for the light, it is already there, pressing up against the curtains, seeking a way in.

Most of us find that if we sit still for twenty minutes our mind goes blank or fills up with immediate concerns, and we need some kind of aid or focal point if we are to arrive at this awareness of the presence. An example of such a focal point is the 'Jesus prayer' which is taught in the Orthodox Church, and which consists in saying again and again one simple phrase, 'Jesus, have mercy.' As this phrase is repeated the mind grows still around it. Many people combine it with breathing slowly in and out, because they understand that this activity of prayer involves the whole of the body as well as of the mind and spirit. 'Jesus, have mercy', breathing in, breathing out. After a short while, the whole rhythm of the mind and body grows slower and quietens.

I once asked a Greek — he was the prior of a monastery perched on top of a rock at Meteora in central Greece — what happened when he repeated this prayer. He told me that he used it at night, in his cell, and then he said, 'First it is me and him, then it becomes him and me. Then it is only him.'

I think he meant something like this.

First it is me and him. I'm thinking about myself. Jesus, have mercy on me. I need your mercy. I am proud and bad-tempered. Jesus, have mercy. I am so frail, so full of anxiety. I am tossed this way and that. Jesus, have mercy. And now

I begin to think of other people, my own family and friends, people I know who are in trouble and who are sick. Jesus, have mercy. I think of the world around me, and how beautiful it is, and how sensitive people are, yet what cruel things they do to each other. I think of people lonely and starving and being tortured. Jesus, have mercy. So I approach the Son of Man, and lift up the whole world into his compassion.

First it is me and him, then it becomes him and me. Gradually I begin to be aware of his presence. Jesus, born in a stable, you know what it is to be poor. Have mercy. Jesus, growing up as a child, who went to school and practised as a carpenter, you know what it is to be like us, have mercy. Jesus, who healed the sick and taught us about compassion, have mercy. Jesus, who broke the bread and allowed yourself to be broken, who hung on the cross, and cried out in the darkness of despair, you know what it is to suffer, have mercy. Jesus, who died and went down to hell, who rose again on the third day, and who promised to come and be with us and in us, have mercy. So as we focus more and more on him, on one aspect or another of the Son of Man, we come to understand that he is approaching us, we recognize the richness of his mercy, and how it embraces the whole of what we are, and how everything we can ever do is held in his heart, and how he understands and has compassion on us.

First it is me and him, then it becomes him and me. Then it is only him. As we say this prayer again and again, we begin to see the world through his eyes. We begin to look through the eyes of the risen Christ – or is he looking through our eyes? – and we see how all things are held together by him in a perfect harmony. Now the words, 'Jesus, have mercy', are no longer a cry for help, they are a glad recognition. 'Jesus, you are having mercy.' We begin to understand how good and evil are part of his creation, and how they are being understood and accepted and forgiven. Then it is only him, because I am no longer at the centre of the picture. My selfish and frightened little ego has become part of his great pattern, part of the communion of all things in heaven and earth. We are caught up out of ourselves to see things in a new way. We understand that the purpose of the whole creation is not to be achieved through our cleverness, or through anything we can plan to do, but only through his compassion and forgiveness by which we are made one. Jesus, mercy. We are conscious with the consciousness of Christ which flows through us. Our prayer is 'in his name'. All we can do is be still with an unconditional relaxation through which his peace can be present, and with a total self-abandonment through which his power can flow. Jesus, mercy . . . and then to pass beyond even those two tiny words into a silence, which is full of his glory and our gratitude.

There is no road-map for the way of contemplation, and the journey will be different for each of us. But some such rhythm as this seems to be the rhythm of the journey repeated every day, and at every stage of our lives at a deeper level. We will look at it more closely.

First it is me and him. Prayer springs spontaneously out of what we really want and feel, as in moments of great danger or great joy. There is no need to be ashamed of this. We have been told to ask, and seek, and knock, and to persevere and go on asking and seeking and knocking. The reason for persevering is not that God is asleep and we have to attract his attention, or that he is unwilling and we have to persuade him to change his mind. It is rather that we may come to a more accurate self-knowledge, with deeper awareness of our own ambiguity, and a keener sense of our own need. The prodigal son 'came to himself', and it was in the moment that he understood his own absolute need that he decided to go home and ask his father for help. This sense of need, as we saw earlier, is the keynote of Jesus' teaching in the Sermon on the Mount, when he reveals to his intimate group of disciples the style of life by which they will enter the new age. 'Blessed are the poor in Spirit,' he says (or, as the New English Bible translates it in its second edition, 'How blest are those who know their need of God'), 'theirs is the kingdom of heaven.' They are already in the new age. They have discovered that what they really want is the presence of God, and as they ask for it, it is already granted. The curtain is drawn back, and the light is already flooding into the room.

Then it becomes him and me. The light is flooding into the room. Now the command is no longer 'Ask', but 'Receive the gift of God's Spirit, for which you have asked.' It is no longer 'Seek', but 'Rejoice because you have been found – the one you thought you were looking for has been looking for you.' It is no longer 'Knock', but 'Open the door of your own heart. You thought you were knocking on God's door, while all the time he has been knocking on yours.'

Now the living water is springing out of the belly, the divine Spirit flowing through the human spirit.

> Thee, God, I come from, to thee go,
> All day long I like fountain flow.[1]

Now we are being given the Christ consciousness, that we come from God and are going to God, beloved sons and daughters of the Abba Father, through whom flows the river of grace and compassion.

But this state of awareness is not yet the fullness of contemplation. All the great religious traditions tell us that it is only an antechamber to the presence. Vimala Thakar, the Hindu mystic, speaking in June 1974 at the New Era Centre, called it a condition of 'psychic puberty' – we are still in a state of duality, where I am the observer observing my own awareness. The ego knows 'the grace is upon me', and this is therefore a moment of great danger – the danger that I should tie up my experience into a theory, and become a crusader who wants to manipulate, teach and convert others. We have to pass, she said, into 'a condition of unconditional relaxation' where I am no more aware that I am aware of the unity of life, 'an unconditional surrender before the mystery of life', to a humility which knows that I do not understand, and which then surrenders even the awareness of my own limitations and weaknesses. We pass from the ego-consciousness to the It-consciousness.

Then it is only him. The Hindu mystic calls it the It-consciousness. The Christian monk speaks rather of a Him-consciousness. No longer 'I am conscious of him', or even 'he is conscious of me', but simply 'he is conscious.' Love is conscious. Love conceives an idea and utters a word and creates a universe. The ego is no longer a little fortified, independent, self-conscious island, but a word which love is uttering, in the poetry which is his creation,

> . . . where every word is at home,
> Taking its place to support the others, . . .
> The complete consort dancing together.[2]

The ego is lost, and the true self is being found in an interdependence with the divine love and with all created things. This true self is not confined by space, or limited by time, or annihilated by death.

> Stretch or contract me thy poore debter:
> This is but tuning of my breast,
> To make the musick better.
> Whether I flie with angels, fall with dust,
> Thy hands made both, and I am there:
> Thy power and love, my love and trust
> Make one place ev'ry where.[3]

One place everywhere and one timeless present, which embrace the past and the future, the material universe, and 'heaven'. The author of some remarkable books on Russian spirituality, Julia de Beausobre, wrote to me at the time of my wife's death: 'I have long felt (and I am not alone in feeling) that since the years of the last war there has been a great shift in the relationship between us and the souls of the dead, between the carnal world and the spiritual. No shift can, of course, be so momentous as was Christ's descent into hell, yet this one is very significant, however elusive. We, who linger on, now know so much more about them who have shed their carnality; and they understand so much more about us (carnal ones) than was generally possible in the nineteenth century. The interaction is at times stupendous. But our understanding of it flows unevenly.'

This arresting idea is not so improbable as it might seem at first sight. During the last thirty years there has opened up to the human race the possibility of a deeper knowledge of nature and of man – and by knowledge I mean not mastering through the intellect but knowing through love (which includes the intellect). If nature/man/God are three distinct aspects of a single reality then should we not expect a similar opening up of the possibility of 'knowing' God – that what has been the privilege of a few pioneer mystics may become the common heritage of us all? If we are approaching an evolutionary leap into a new complexity which embraces past, present and future, then might it be in the direction of that ultimate complexity which is communion with 'the whole company of heaven'? If the flash-point of change is a true self consciousness, which includes our willing response to the divine centre, then might the new age involve some rending of the veil between God's mercy and man's sacrifice, as happened at the death of Jesus, some step towards the ultimate reign of the divine love 'on earth as it is in heaven'. The two meanings of *zoë aionios* – 'the life of the new age' and 'eternal life' – come together to describe that quality of life which the Son of Man sets free in men.

But this resurrection life can only come through death. This new consciousness is a free gift which comes through the death and resurrection of the total reality of myself/ the other/God. When someone dies whom we have loved, they are lifted out of the interplay of human fallibilities, and now from beyond death they come to us with an unambiguous freedom which lifts us both into a new dimension of relationship.

We die with the dying:
See, they depart, and we go with them.
We are born with the dead:
See, they return, and bring us with them.[4]

For Christians this human experience is focused in the risen Christ who has passed through the ultimate point where good and evil interlock, and now through the interaction of faith he comes to us with unambiguous forgiveness – setting free in us the courage to know ourselves, to have compassion, and to respond to the divine centre.

This is the contemplative life, to be lived when we have passed through the antechamber of contemplative prayer. I once asked the Mother General of an order of contemplative nuns, 'What is this life which you are leading?' and she replied, 'It is to stand with Christ where good and evil interlock.'

That is, to stand with Christ who was crucified and now is risen. As always he says to us, 'Do not cling to me.' This new consciousness is not something you can understand and put into words today in order to make use of it tomorrow. It is only yours now, in this timeless present. You can make no images to express it, for the divine love cannot be limited by any image. Not that! Not that! You can only be silent. All images must be broken, so that the truth towards which they pointed may flow through you. A spring of living water? No, not that! That symbol will no longer serve though it has helped us so far along the way. I am the Way. Now it is only him, and even he must be broken. The water must be turned into wine – his life-blood, given to us, his joy springing out of us in the mutual give and take of love.

And as for ourselves:

Quick now, here, now, always –
A condition of complete simplicity
(Costing not less than everything).[5]

This chapter is an attempt to show how contemplation forms one aspect of the threefold style of the new Church of the new age. It is not a handbook on the practice of contemplative prayer. Nevertheless, because the crisis is upon us, it would perhaps be helpful to indicate the lines along which we could take these insights into our practice both of private prayer and public worship.

PRIVATE PRAYER

We pray with the body as well as with the mind, and the posture of the body can either express or deny the truth of our encounter with God. If we are lolling in an arm-chair with crossed legs, this is not expressing the eager expectation that out of the present moment the divine love is coming towards us with an absolute forgiveness and an absolute demand. We may kneel, or lie prostrate with arms spread out, or sit on a chair erect with our feet on the floor and our head, neck and spine in a straight line. The eastern position of sitting cross-legged on the floor is being more generally adopted in the West, because it ex-presses the in-folding of the whole person upon the centre from which the spring of the spirit is to flow.

Exercises can keep the body flexible, and so encourage a flexibility of spirit. By the way we stand we can express stability. By the way we walk we can express the conscious-ness that we carry the divine centre within the centre of ourselves, and that we are moving with total awareness towards a goal. By slow rhythmic breathing we can help our bodies and minds to relax and grow quiet.

Concentration. God is hidden within his creation, and by concentrating on one detail of it we may become aware of his presence. This detail may be a word, or a phrase such as the 'Jesus prayer' of the Orthodox Church. It may be a symbol, such as a lighted candle, or a cross, or a loaf of bread. If we are Christians we shall choose a symbol which points to some aspect of Christ, who is the light of the world, the resurrection, the bread of life. Such sym-bols have infinite depths of meaning, and as we concentrate upon them we are led towards the reality which they symbolize.

Meditation.

(i) We use our intellect upon the object of our concentration – the word, the phrase, the symbol – probing, discriminating, understanding. For example, we may think of light, the sources of light, the uses of light, and grow in awareness of Christ the light of the world.

(ii) But then, after a while, we must allow this understanding to move from our head to our heart so that we accept the truth we have been thinking about into our lives. We accept the light of the world into our darkness, to illuminate and reveal.

(iii) Beyond that again, we offer ourselves so that the light may shine through us, and we may carry it 'to those who walk in darkness and in the shadow of death'.

This threefold pattern of meditation was taught by St Francis de Sales as 'Christ in the eyes, Christ in the heart, Christ in the hands .

Contemplation. So far, the prayer we have described has seemed to be more or less under our own control. It is something we appear to initiate. But as we pass to contemplation (and sometimes we may be allowed to jump straight into contemplation without any of these preliminaries) it becomes apparent that the initiative is with God. What we have symbolized, what we have been thinking about, takes possession of us and flows through us. As somebody once put it to me, 'I no longer pray prayer, but prayer prays me.'

When this happens, it is a free gift. Then we can have done with words, and simply allow God to be present, and for our part be still and be thankful. But this stillness has also the nature of a flow. When a physicist tries to describe the reality he is investigating, he may talk of the paradox of a steady state inside a flow; so the one who is caught up into contemplation finds himself using the same paradox to describe the spiritual reality which he experiences. The presence flows through him, and in this flow he intercedes for others. He is no longer trying to attract God's attention and to enlist his support, he is allowing the divine love to flow out through him and to touch and be present with another person. I/the other/God are together in the eternal stillness and flowing of the present moment.

But the awareness of the presence will itself have to be broken. 'Do not cling to me.' The Pentecostal experience of the gushing of the Spirit must die, and be raised again and received afresh as a new gift at an even deeper level. For much of the journey we are aware only of the absence. But it is at these moments when the traveller seems to himself to be groping about in the darkness, that others may see the radiance shining around him. He himself, in the cloud of unknowing, knows only his need for God – but that is all he needs to know. In that instant, the kingdom of God is already his, and in his weakness there is entrusted to him the sovereign power of the divine forgiveness.

PUBLIC WORSHIP
Public worship is of ultimate significance. There is a Latin proverb, 'As you pray, so you will believe' (*Lex orandi lex credendi*). As we act out our ritual, we are expressing the secrets of our own hearts. We are articulating what we believe about ourselves (the whole reality of nature/man/God), bringing it up into consciousness so that we can say, 'Aha! Now I understand what I am.'

Modern urban society has lost the old rituals which were bound to the rhythms of nature and at the same time to a belief in God, such as Christmas and Easter and the harvest festival. We try to fill the vacuum with other rituals, such as the cup final and the pop festival. But now the leap forward into a new complexity demands that, like an orchestra of highly individualistic players responding together to the conductor, we learn to act out together the truth of our interdependence and of our response to the divine centre.

Silence. For the Christian Church, this means that we

must move towards a worship which is more contemplative. It must lead us into silence, because any words about God are in the end a kind of blasphemy which limits him. The Quakers can teach us about a silence which is not an emptiness, but which is full of communion, so that through the silence we come closer to each other, and experience the divine love coming closer to us, than through the use of words.

Words. But words have their preliminary use as an approach to silence, provided they are understood not as defining and grasping hold of the truth, but as pointing towards the truth by which we will then be grasped.

When the disciples asked Jesus to teach them to pray, he gave them words, but words which reveal a fuller richness if they are understood in this contemplative mode.

Abba (Father). He, the Father, is running towards us in compassion. We say the word so that our eyes may be opened to this truth.

Thy name be hallowed. The whole creation is declaring his name (his character). It is singing the song of his glory, and we are part of that music. To say the words is to draw back the curtains, and the light has already filled the room.

Thy kingdom come. It is coming, through millions of years, through evolution, through individual acts of kindness, through the acceptance of suffering, through good and evil interlocked and transformed by death and resurrection. As we say the words, we abandon ourselves to the purpose so that it may flow through us. 'Thy will be done, on earth as in heaven.'

Give us each day our daily bread. As we ask, we unblock the channels through which his gifts may be given. He cares more than we do about the needs of men, both for physical bread and for the divine bread. We open ourselves to the absolute demands of his compassion.

Forgive us our sins, for we too forgive all who are in debt to us. As the sovereign power of forgiveness flows through us in the timeless moment, we are already accepted, our failures are transformed, those who have failed us are partners with us in the new age.

Do not bring us to the test, but save us from evil. Here is the ultimate cry of our weakness, and the ultimate expression of the Father's power. Do not bring us to our breaking point, but if we must be broken, then in that hour protect us, hold us safe, from the evil one.

As with each phrase in this great prayer, *first it is me and him, then it is him and me.* Now the hour of my weakness has come and as I walk through the valley of the shadow of death, thou art with me. *Then it is only him.* After the words, silence. The truth towards which they have pointed.

The flow. 'The time approaches,' said Jesus, 'indeed it is already here, when those who are real worshippers will worship the Father in Spirit and in truth.' The Spirit will leap out of their bellies and flow through them.

Flowing water has to come in and it has to go out. When a company of people are worshipping together, the Spirit comes in through their love for each other – if there is no love, there can be no Spirit. But it goes out through their concern for the kingdom of God, that is to say that the sovereign power of love shall prevail in some area of life. If the water comes in but cannot get out then there is a stagnant pool, and this is the condition of some Christian communities who care for each other but shut out the concerns of the world around them. If the water flows out but it is not replenished, then there is a dry mud patch, and this is the condition of some activist groups who have no time to give to each other. For the Spirit to flow, the balance must be maintained.

The truth of this has been experienced by all of us in acts of public worship. We pray at the beginning of our service that the worship may be 'in Spirit'.

> Almighty God, unto whom all hearts be open
> all desires known,
> and from whom no secrets are hid;

> Cleanse the thoughts of our hearts by the
> inspiration of thy Holy Spirit,
> that we may perfectly love thee,
> and worthily magnify thy Holy Name.

But if our hearts are shut towards each other, our desires unmentionable, our secrets hidden, then there can be no inspiration of Holy Spirit. The Spirit enters through our human love.

Many groups today are beginning to express this love for each other – this interdependence – and to find that it grows through being expressed. They sit so that they can see each other. They are not afraid to touch, to embrace. Here and there, tentatively, they are beginning to dance, so returning to the most ancient form of worship which involves the whole body and our interaction with each other in movement. Where such things are being done, many are experiencing a new reality of worship.

But there is always the danger that this experience of worship is no more than the gushing in of emotion. The Spirit must also flow out through a concern which we share or a purpose to which we are committed. To take a very ordinary example, a minister is leading the prayers, and the attention of the congregation is wandering – then he mentions somebody who is sick, whom we all love. Suddenly, we wake up, the Spirit of prayer grasps hold of us, and flows out through our common concern. This happens also in moments of common thanksgiving and dedication.

The Sacrament. The way of contemplation was acted out by Jesus at the Last Supper. To eat a meal with a group of friends is a natural and universal expression of human love, and on that particular occasion the company sitting round the table had arrived together at a crisis of common concern. In the flow of the Spirit, flowing in through their love, flowing out through their concern.

Jesus took bread. He concentrated upon a symbol. Bread is a symbol with an infinite depth of meaning, which includes the mystery of death and resurrection. Before the wheat can row, the seed has to 'fall into the ground and die'.[6] Its hard shell has to be broken by the new life, pushing out from inside it to be born. Then the wheat in its turn must die — at the moment of its ripeness it is cut down, threshed, ground into flour. The flour, leavened with yeast, becomes the living, rising dough, but when it has risen to the critical point it too must die — it is thrust into the oven, so that it may emerge from the heat as bread which is able to feed the bodies of men and women.

He gave thanks. As Jesus took the bread into his hands, the actual words he used were probably those of the Hebrew blessing before meals, 'Blessed be thou, O Lord God, King of the Universe, who bringest forth bread from the earth.' Within the natural creation he saw the creator. In the bread he saw the pattern of God's dealing with men. He saw also himself and the death he must die, and he said, 'This is my body.' Through the symbol he recognized the truth towards which it pointed, the threefold reality of nature/man/God, and within that reality his own true self as the grace flowed through him in a moment of self-knowledge, compassion, and willing obedience to God.

He broke it. All symbols have to be broken in order that the truth towards which they point may grasp hold of us. The body of Jesus had to be broken, and he himself to go out beyond the self-consciousness of grace, so that the unambiguous love might flow through him.

He gave it. 'Take, eat.' He gave himself to his friends, in an act of self-abandonment to them and to God. This gift of *himself* would become in them the fountain of the Spirit, springing up out of the depths of *themselves*.

Then he said, 'Do this in remembrance of me.' The Greek word for remembrance does not mean 'cast your mind back into the past', but 'call the past into the present.' When you re-enact the breaking of the bread, do not think back nostalgically to our past life together. As you remember me, be aware that now, today, in the timelessness of the present moment, I am remembering you. I am coming to you. Clear the way, remove the obstacles, so that I may be with you. Be full of gratitude. Let your 'selves' be broken so that I may be in you your 'true selves'. Then we shall know together what is beyond knowledge, the Christ consciousness, 'I am the resurrection and the life', the divine love, the joy and the peace of the new age.

There were thirteen people sitting at that table – which brings us to the subject of the next chapter.

8. *The Group*

The leap forward into complexity will demand of us that we belong at the same time to larger groups and to smaller groups.

In the secular world this double movement is already happening. As we noticed in chapter 6, within the great multinational corporations and anonymous cities of our time small groups are deliberately being structured, or are emerging spontaneously, where people can be personally known. Similarly the new style of the Church, while it will include at international and national level centres of prayer and pilgrimage, of research, training and administration, will at the same time involve its individual members in small groups or cells. The great centres may help us to catch the vision of one world and one reality, but it is the small group which provides the womb out of which the true self can most naturally come to birth, and where complexity, forgiveness, the life of the new age, can most readily be experienced and learnt.

We will begin with some of the earthy facts of group life, and then proceed to the quality of the new consciousness which they engender. This chapter is not a text-book on group dynamics, but contains some modest suggestions of how the understanding of group life, which has grown over the last generation, illuminates the Christian truth, and how the Christ event gives strength to the group process. 'Group dynamics' has become a sort of mystery cult, with priests and oracles and arcane knowledge, whereas the term only describes 'what goes on in groups', and this is something which everybody has experienced who belongs to a family or to any working group. It is something which cannot be avoided, and is therefore much better understood, so that we can use it positively instead of allowing it to push us around.

There can be no blueprint for group work, because every group is different from every other. It is important that this simple and obvious fact be appreciated. The genetic endowment of every human being is different, his finger prints are different, the shape of his stomach is different. How much more must we expect each group to be different, where a number of human beings are reacting to each other with all the criss-cross of their personalities – to say nothing of the influence of the particular day and hour in which they meet, the weather, the headlines in the newspapers, and the multifarious predicaments of each group member, with his or her joys and griefs, irritations and hopes. Any conductor of such a group who thinks to himself, 'I know how to handle this situation – such and such a technique worked last time', is heading for disaster. He must be sensitive to what is happening *this* time.

But there are certain rhythms and patterns which are common to groups.

THE SIZE OF THE GROUP

Size affects the quality of relationships. For example, in a group of twelve or under each member can relate personally to every other, and can engage in discussion. When the number rises to twenty, the members begin to address a public meeting, and no longer to give and take in conversation. From two to five is the best size for a deep, intimate, creative shaping of ideas. A large group of fifty and upwards seems to be capable of a different quality of experience, which in its malignant form becomes mass hysteria, but in its healthy form can enable in its members a deep conviction of truth, joy, peace and love. For the Christian Church these elementary facts and figures should be understood as the framework within which spiritual renewal takes place. Christ himself said, 'When two or three are gathered together in my name, there am I in the midst of them.' This suggests that the kind of contemplative prayer which we described in the last chapter, 'in his name', will normally be a gift given to a small group. When Jesus needed to abandon himself in prayer at the great turning points of his life he seems to have invited three special friends to come with him. They accompanied him to the mountain where he was transfigured, and where he shone with the glory of the presence as he chose the way of death, and again to the garden of Gethsemane where the sweat rolled off him like drops of blood, as he accepted death and moved into an identification with his Father's will. At each of these great contemplative moments he had, in the event, to stand alone, because his friends were not able to share this prayer with him, but he needed them even if they could not understand. His true self needed to be held and strengthened by their love.

Similarly he chose a group of twelve 'disciples' who were to become 'apostles'. These two words indicate first that they were 'learners', and secondly that they would be sent out' to perform a task. A group of twelve is the optimum size to encourage these two elements of group life at one and the same time, namely the growth of each individual member and the carrying out of a group task. But it is also the right size for a third element which in this case was of overriding importance – the interchange between the members, and their discovery of forgiveness. It cannot be over-emphasized that the prototype of the Christian Church was a group of twelve people, who ate and talked together, argued and quarrelled, and were finally overwhelmed with the experience of forgiveness, which was itself the message they had to carry to the whole human race. They could not carry it before they had experienced it, and they could not experience it except in a group where tensions were actually built up and resolved, where personalities actually clashed, where weakness was revealed and accepted and transformed into strength. It is not simply ironic, it is tragic, that the typical meeting of the Christian Church has become the gathering of a large congregation, with the assumption that the larger the congregation the greater the success. In this

age of anonymous urban man, when we begin to doubt
the value of hugeness, and to wonder whether after all the
'small is beautiful', the Christian Church must rediscover
its original smallness and the intimacy through which its
members can learn the interdependence and love which is the
life of the new age. This it will be more able to do if its
typical structure is the small group, where people have the
opportunity to clash with each other and to experience
forgiveness.

But this is not to say that there should be no large
group meetings. The one does not exclude the other, but
on the contrary demands it. As everywhere else, good and
evil are interlocked in the dynamics of a small group,
which can give birth to the best but also to the worst – it can
become the place of love but also the place of bitter hatred,
a creative power-house or a sterile clique. A proper balance
demands that we also meet in large assemblies, perhaps
in great buildings and open-air festivals where our minds
can be lifted out of our immediate concerns into a vision of
our unity with all created things, where trumpets can sound
or a silence fall on a multitude of people, so that for a
moment we catch a glimpse of joy that is beyond human
understanding. We need also to meet in large groups of
up to a hundred and twenty, which is thought by the Institute of Group Analysis in London to be the maximum
number of people who can share a cohesive group experience.
It is worth noting that there were about a hundred and
twenty people present on the day of Pentecost, when they
became aware of the rushing wind of the Spirit, and the
central fire of the presence which divided and lighted upon
each one of them in a tongue of flame. On that day they were
caught up into the threefold experience by which each one
becomes more truly himself, is at the same time united
with others, and responds to a single divine centre. Large
groups of a hundred and twenty, in contrast to small groups
of twelve, can mediate to us a different experience of the
Spirit, perhaps more powerful, more overwhelming. But
for this to be positive and creative and not to deteriorate into

mass hysteria there needs to be a firm framework of ritual, or somebody who is confidently in control, so that the forces which are let loose shall be for healing and not for destruction.

THE SHAPE OF THE GROUP

Shape also affects relationships. If a small group of people are to share their thoughts and feelings, then they do best to seat themselves in such a way that they can see each other, and are on the same level. This may mean sitting on the floor, or on chairs of equal height. If they sit round a table, then the table also affects their relationships – it can help them to perform a practical task, but it can also divide them so that they find it more difficult to be open with each other. Often some members of a group will insist on having a table, which enables them to hide behind it and to feel safe from the threats of the other members, but if they can be persuaded to do without it, the mutual trust within the group may be increased. People often feel in alliance with those whom they are sitting beside, and in opposition to those whom they are sitting opposite. It would seem, therefore, that the shape of a group may be of more significance than we generally suppose.

But again, there is no blueprint. A few years ago I organized a conference on the theme of prayer, and arranged for sessions of meditation to take place in a little chapel. In order that we might be more united, I broke up the rows of chairs and formed them into a circle, which in those days was quite a radical move. After we had finished our meditation, one of the young people present asked, 'Why did we have to sit in that rigid circle?' So for the next session we invited each person to take up any position they wished in the chapel. Some sat on chairs, placing the chair wherever they liked. Some sat cross-legged. Others knelt, stood, or lay prostrate on the floor. The result was an astonishing experience of unity and the removal of barriers. Each one was expressing himself or herself, and yet with an awareness of the others, and in a common response to the divine love.

The same is true in the large groups. Congregations are used to sitting in rows, and responding with a semi-military precision to orders issuing from the minister who stands in front of them. On the command 'Let us pray', each worshipper kneels or slumps forward or bows his head according to his ecclesiastical tradition. There are signs of a welcome revolt and that people are feeling free to adopt their own position – which could be an outward sign of an inner movement from dependence through independence and towards a fuller interdependence.

There is also a growing tendency to sit or stand in such a way that people are able to see and enjoy each other. This may be in a circle, or if the group is larger in concentric circles. The ultimate large group, which Dante saw in his vision of Paradise, was the whole company of the saints in heaven seated in concentric circles so that they together formed the shape of a rose, and each person whom the divine Spirit had kindled into his own unique self-hood was now united with the others in a symbol of perfect beauty.

THE PHASES OF A GROUP
Groups often follow a long-term pattern which is expressed diagrammatically by Richard Hauser like this:

There is a first phase when the group is enthusiastic and creative, and working out its purpose. This is followed by a second phase when it operates efficiently, and by a third phase during which it declines. When this third phase is reached, the group ought to be disbanded, or else should rethink and reformulate its purpose, and start again on a new upward creative phase. An example is the Mothers' Union, which was launched with the creative purpose of being a band of mothers in every community who would promote the ideal of family life, pray together, and support each other. (This bears the threefold stamp of renewal which we have described earlier.) After a time the Mothers' Union began to lose this creative quality, and became an efficient organization of women who served the Church in many practical ways. After a further period they became a rump (or a network of rumps) of elderly ladies whose preoccupation appeared to those outside to be their own survival, and the exclusion of any woman who had been divorced. Then again, after a long and painful rethink, they courageously altered their own constitution, and are now hopefully launching out once more with a new flexibility, and a vision of how they may be true to their original purpose in a changed world where that vision is more than ever needed.

Within this long-term pattern, and often during a single meeting, groups may follow another pattern to which we have had cause to refer many times, the pattern of dependence/independence/interdependence. This is the normal development of every human life, as the child grows through adolescence and into responsible adulthood, but we find it re-enacted within a group situation, where it has to be lived through again and again. Each of us contains within himself the child, the adolescent and the adult, and these elements in our personality can be activated by a situation which involves our relation to other people and to authority. Thus we find a group of adults, newly arrived at a conference where they do not know each other or the chairman and staff, acting like children with an exaggerated dependence and obedience. After a while they are quite likely to challenge the platform, or to become worked up about some detail of administration in a way which is out of all proportion to its importance. They may insist on some change in the programme, but once they have won a victory and made their mark and discovered that the chairman is fallible, they will settle down to work together as responsible adults. In some mysterious way, the group has to relive this universal pattern of human development in order to grow itself.

But this pattern is also, on a macro-scale, the story of the development of the human race – from a dependence on the tribe (mother) to dependence on the king (father) to the independence and individualism of the Renaissance (adolescence) to the interdependence which is demanded of us today (adulthood). If a group is the context in which this essential process can be repeatedly experienced and understood, then we begin to understand how it could be the school of self-knowledge, where we learn the secret of complexity and enable the evolutionary leap.

But this self-knowledge is gained at cost, and the cost is first of all to be borne by the leader.

LEADERSHIP IN THE GROUPS

The leader must be aware of these processes, and must enable the groups to pass through them and so to develop and grow. This means that his style of leadership must be on a sliding scale which is illustrated in the following diagram.

Authority retained

Authority shared

At one end of the scale he must be prepared to exercise an almost autocratic authority. The reason for this may be either that the group are feeling and behaving like children, and need to be told what to do, or that there is a crisis situation such as an outbreak of fire which allows no time to consult. As we move up the scale we find the leader first explaining his decisions to the group, then asking for their opinions and discussing the question at issue, and finally leaving the decision in their hands. But the diagram shows that some modicum of authority has always to be retained, and some to be shared. Even in a battle, when the military commander shouts to his troops, 'Charge!' he relies on their trust in himself, or at least their loyalty to the system he represents – as in the extreme case of the charge of the Light Brigade.

> Theirs not to reason why,
> Theirs but to do and die.[1]

At the other end of the scale, authority cannot be totally abdicated. The leader may be doing no more than articulate the decision of the group, but this in itself can require patience, subtlety, humility, and the ability to reconcile differences. It may be a more skilful and exacting type of leadership than that of the autocrat.

In moving from one style of leadership to another, as the group advances towards adulthood or regresses towards childhood, the leader may have to bear a lot of pain. The members of the groups may project on to him their own fear and aggression, their guilt or self-hatred. They may attack him for something which they fear or dislike in themselves – and because the leader is human, they are probably right in spotting this weakness in him. The leader, therefore, cannot simply sit back and think to himself, 'Now they are acting like adolescents attacking their father, but of course the fault is in them not in me.' He must rather think, 'the fault is also in me but because it is in them too they notice it, and dislike it, and touch me on the raw, and I feel pain. But if I can expose myself to their attack, and if I can at the same time help them to understand why they are attacking me, then we can bring up into the light of consciousness another area of human nature which we share together, and we can accept another weakness in ourselves and each other which can be transformed into a strength, or another point of injury which can become a point of healing.'

So the cost must be borne by the leader, but if the healing process is going to take place, then it must also be borne by the members of the group. And here we come to the heart of the matter.

THE GROUP AS THE PLACE FOR FORGIVENESS

(a) *The small group is* par excellence *the place where a person comes to new self-awareness.* This is generally a painful process, and it often happens suddenly and unexpectedly in the give and take of group life. We cannot go on pretending to one another and hiding what we really are, and as we get to know each other there comes perhaps a moment of irritation, perhaps a moment of deep friendship, when somebody lets slip a truth about ourselves. We are stabbed, as light penetrates into a dark place. Often what is revealed to us is something we knew on the intellectual level, but now we suddenly experience it at the emotional level. It hurts, because what is broken is some illusion about ourselves which we have cherished, and which seems to be the *raison d'être* of our being and the mainspring of our activity. Suddenly we are made aware of the dark side of that very virtue on which we prided ourselves. It is the moment in which Perceval's sword broke in the fight with Orguelleus, and when he discovered that the best thing in him was also the worst. It is the moment of disillusion, the moment when I discover how ordinary and earthy I am. The moment in which Elijah prayed that he might die, 'For' he said, 'I am no better than my fathers.'

Of course disillusion is in the end healthy, because to live under an illusion is both harmful to ourselves and destructive to other people. But the moment of disillusion is dangerous, and is generally followed by depression, and can lead to the feeling that I am falling apart and losing control. At such a moment I need to be supported by the group, and particularly by the leader of the group – held together, as it were, so that I can let myself fall apart, and come face to face with a new area of my own ambivalence, and accept it, and find a new integration of myself round a new centre of truth. This is a kind of death and rebirth, a crisis in which the interlocking of good and evil is transformed by death and resurrection.

To become aware of my own ambivalence will mean, for example, to understand that I love what I hate and hate what I love, or that I am at the same time and for the same reason sensitive and insensitive to other people, or that I have chosen my career to cover up my own feeling of inadequacy. A psychiatrist put me wise to this truth one day as I travelled with him in a train, and during our conversation he admitted to me that he had become a psychiatrist because he knew himself to be a mixed-up kid. But it was not till ten years later that I came to know emotionally that this also applied to me, and that I had become a clergyman because I found it difficult to love people. Such discoveries are often made, and are best made, in the context of a supporting and loving group, who can help one to see that this terrible weakness is also one's greatest strength. The psychiatrist, for example, was a very good psychiatrist, much respected and sought after, and the fact that he knew himself to be a mixed-up kid had driven him to wrestle with his own problems and research into and uncover his own phobias, and then to understand and accept them, so that he had become a man of exceptional authority and compassion in this very field. The same thing is true of someone who is physically handicapped, and who has been able to transform his liability into his chief asset.

Such new self-awareness shared with others can lead the member of a group to the astonishing discovery that when his weakness is known he is accepted in spite of it, and indeed loved even more because of it. In face of this amazing paradox he may begin to have the courage to accept himself, and even to love himself, as he discovers a new freedom which comes out of his disillusion and the stripping off of his pretences, and a new reality and compassion in his dealings with other people.

(b) *Self-awareness goes hand in hand with awareness of others,* and so it is that in the life of a small group we discover the depth and complexity of our relations with other people. The group develops a personality of its own, and has moods, so that one day it will be sullen and fractious, and on another free and communicative. The members become aspects of this composite personality, and the group acting as a whole seems to assign roles to each, so that one is set up as the joker, another as the mother, another as the counsellor. It is as though all the functions of a human cell or family have to be performed, and if one member leaves another will pick up the role that he or she has been playing. As we experience this group life we become aware that human beings flow in and out of one another. We are not individuals, not like billiard balls which bump against one another, but part of an organic cell — we interact, interlock and interplay with each other. At a deep level we seem to be open to one another. The prayer to 'Almighty God, to whom all hearts be open, all desires known and from whom no secrets are hid', appears to describe our relations to each other. We cannot hide. An angry thought wounds, even though it is not expressed, and a caring thought builds up and supports. It is through the life of a small group that we come to know in our guts what we have already accepted in our heads, that we and others are interdependent.

Part of group life is tension, and the clash of personalities. Lord Hunt, then Sir John Hunt, the leader of the first expedition to reach the summit of Mt Everest, said in a lecture on his return home that he chose each member of the team not primarily as an outstanding mountaineer, but as a man who would get on well with his colleagues. You cannot afford to have any lurking irritation between two climbers who are cutting steps up a glacier at twenty-seven thousand feet.

You cannot, however, avoid it. Every good group or team which is going to be creative, as indeed every good marriage, must experience the clash of personalities. This is so painful that many groups disband, and return to the simpler style of operating as individuals. But if they can face their own ambiguity — the betrayals which go hand in hand with their loyalty to each other — if they can dare to express their anger and despair to each other, then they may be led through an experience of death and resurrection by which the good and evil within them may be unlocked.

Then they may begin to discriminate, and to understand how the evil in one activates the evil in the other, but that at a deeper level there is a reality and a timeless present in which the true self of the one is united to the true self of the other.

> And all shall be well and
> All manner of thing shall be well
> When the tongues of flame are in-folded
> Into the crowned knot of fire
> And the fire and the rose are one.[2]

Out of such an experience of forgiveness, which may be on a little scale and often repeated, they can arrive at a new understanding of their interdependence. It is no longer as though the bits of knowledge and insight which each one brought into the group had been fitted together like pieces of a jigsaw puzzle, but rather there is a new quality of understanding as though all the bits have entered into each other like tongues of flame into a single fire. Now the group is entering together into the knowledge of the new age, and what St Paul prayed for is coming true. 'That you may understand, with all the saints, what is the breadth and length and height and depth of the love of Christ, and to know it though it surpasses knowledge.'

They are becoming, at the same time, a group who can enable the evolutionary leap into the new age, because they are themselves the ferment of the new quality of life which can permeate their environment, as much by what they are as by anything that they may say and do.

(c) *The third factor in this experience of forgiveness is coming to terms with authority and with the leadership of the group.* This will be embodied in an individual leader, and at the same time be exercised by the group as a whole.

Relationship to authority is one of the basic human problems, and it must be worked through (and at least partly resolved) by any person who is developing from the ego to the true self, as well as by any group who is developing towards the life of the new age. Authority is necessary if any creative advance is to be made – for example, an artist must have a frame within which he paints a picture, otherwise he cannot balance one form and colour against another to create a work of art. A child can develop more healthily against a background of known rules, which give him security against which to experiment (even if the experiment is to break the rules), and an assurance of his parents' love – for if they did not love him, they would not bother to impose rules. Similarly, an adult can take risks (even the risk of losing control of himself) if he knows he is supported by some overarching or undergirding authority, which will not 'let him go' or 'let him down'.

A new leader generally enjoys a honeymoon of goodwill, because people know instinctively that they need authority. Then, inevitably, the leader becomes a problem because authority is a problem. From adulation his followers may change suddenly to denigration. He was their ideal, their fantasy, their illusion of the perfect father or godlike hero, and suddenly he is revealed to them in all his fallibility as a human being. The group (be it large or small) gossips together over the fascinating topic of his strengths and weaknesses, and begins to attack him publicly, but with apologies and protestations of loyalty. There is one school of thought which sees the whole behaviour of the group in terms of this ambiguous reaction to authority, and there seems to be at least this truth in their theory, that authority is one strand which is plaited together with the other two (of self-knowledge and personal relations) to make the internal and on-going life of the group.

The leader can react in a number of ways. He can focus the attention of the group upon its purpose, and thus relieve the pressure on himself. He can make warm personal relationships with each individual member of the group, while retaining his command over the group as a whole. Both these tactics may be beneficial and promote the health of the group. But if he aspires to enable the group to live the life of the new age, then alongside and in conjunction with these two styles of leadership he must adopt a third, which is to be one step ahead of the group in this very process of forgiveness which is its essence. That is to say, he must become more aware of the good and evil that interlock both in himself and in the group, and he must pass through the experience of death and resurrection by which they may be unlocked and transformed. This he will have to do not once, but continuously. As Jesus put it, hyperbolically but realistically, he must 'take up his cross daily'.

Dr A. C. R. Skynner of the Institute of Group Analysis expressed this same idea in psychological terms in a lecture on 'Listening to the Group as a whole' (in the context of therapy). The leader must enter into what the group is thinking and share their confusion. 'It seems to me that what is required . . . is mainly that he try to follow the group theme, and attempt to be aware of conflicts and feelings that it arouses in himself, so that he may allow the increased consciousness provided by the situation to help him solve his own obstacles in facing it. If he does so he will be leading the group (i.e. going ahead and leading the way, rather than encouraging others on from behind which is often substituted for leadership) and his other activities will follow naturally. These are:

(i) clarification of the task the group is working on and

(ii) more important, he must "comprehend" (grasp mentally, have understanding of, be inclusive of, embrace, comprise – Pocket Oxford Dictionary) the group as a whole, and if he can do this probably nothing more is required of him. By "holding" the group in this way he provides a secure container (room to move, time to face things, space to change), within which it is safe to test out new ways of dealing with the world, corresponding to the safe containment and control provided by the mother to the foetus and later to the infant, and by the father to the mother/child complex, and later to the family.'

It is this growth and development within the group which he will be fostering, so that the members may grow in self-confidence and in trust towards each other till they reach a maturity where they can take over responsibility themselves. Then the leader may have to die another death, to go away and to leave them to get on with things in their own way. But this may also become an experience of resurrection, for when the leader is gone the other members of the group may feel free from the ambiguities of their relation to his authority, and free for the first time to adopt *his* way themselves.

These three potentialities of growth are present in every small group – whether it be a group of workers in industry, or of doctors and nurses in a hospital, an ensemble of musicians or a mountaineering expedition – to grow in self-knowledge, awareness of others, and in the acceptance of a true authority. But they are realized more positively, and with less danger to those taking part, when the group is focused upon the presence of Christ, so that they may be experienced by each of the members and by the whole group as his way of forgiveness. The Christian Church has much to learn about group life from professional psychologists, but it also has something to contribute, which is the story and the symbol of an unconditional forgiveness, and the method of articulating and acting it out within a company of people.

THE GROUP AS THE PLACE FOR CONTEMPLATION

We saw in the last chapter that as prayer moves towards contemplation it grows and changes, and finally stands on its head as we discover that it is no longer we who are seeking God, but God who is seeking us. Our part is to abandon ourselves to the divine presence. Now we are ready to state another conclusion, that the organism through which the divine presence can express itself most perfectly is not the individual human being, but the group who are living in the interaction of faith. Contemplation will reach its fullness in such a group, for contemplation is the divine love declaring itself, and the divine love declares itself most naturally through the give and take of our human love.

When we speak of contemplation, we have to distinguish between the contemplative life, and contemplative prayer. The contemplative life is the whole of life lived in response to the divine love, which expresses itself through all that we think and desire and will and do. Contemplative prayer is the special activity, within that life, by which we become aware of the divine love confronting us in the present moment. As the group is the natural channel through which the contemplative life can flow, so it is also the natural context for contemplative prayer.

It is in the small group that we are confronted by the total reality which is myself/the other/God, and where the different aspects of prayer take on a new quality. We can be silent together and come to know each other more profoundly than through words. We can utter our needs, or our thanks, not in lengthy prayers but in a phrase, a mono-syllable – somebody's name or need dropped into the silence, caught up in the flow of the river. We can study together, sharing not only our intellectual ideas, but our imaginative insights. Above all, we can act out the story and the symbol of forgiveness in its original simplicity.

I once belonged to a group of seven who were all concerned with the life of a modern city, trying to discover how a Christian group might be a ferment within the city of this life of the new age. Each was active in his own particular sphere, but we agreed to meet once a week to celebrate the Holy Communion, to eat supper together, and to talk. The first evening we used a simple version of the printed service, and there was a sense of joy and freedom as we passed the bread and wine round to each other in the informality of somebody's living-room. Then we ate supper, and after that we talked. On the second occasion we simplified the ritual, and by the fourth or fifth occasion we had given up any printed book, and each member of the group led one part of the service in his own words.

I think it was on the sixth occasion that my wife and I were hosts, and we said to ourselves, 'How can this gathering become more natural?' because we had a hunch that the supernatural expresses itself through the natural. So we decided to let the evening run in the same rhythm as any other evening when we had guests. We sat down to supper, and enjoyed good food and wine. Then in that lovely moment after supper when people have eaten and drunk and are feeling united, in that moment when the best conversations happen, we agreed that our conversation should be about the best thing – so we read the gospel, and talked about it together for half an hour. Gradually the conversation passed into silence and the silence into prayer. We gave expression to our gratitude, to the needs of the world and our own needs, and in particular our need of forgiveness. Then we declared the presence here and now of that unconditional forgiveness, and embraced each other. Now we were coming to the climax of the service, and I as host found myself breaking bread and taking a cup of wine in my own hands, and to my own astonishment I heard myself saying, 'After supper, he took the cup.'

Yes, of course. After supper! I had never seen it till that moment. In the company of his friends after they had eaten together – in the context of trust, but at the same time of treachery – *at that moment of natural love which is nevertheless always ambiguous he gave the sign of supernatural love,* the sign of his own death and resurrection through which good and evil would be unlocked and the unambiguous love set free.

If I tell this story, it is not in the hope that others will copy what we did. In a sense it is 'copyright'. No one must copy it, because every group is different from every other group, and each must find its own response.

> For the pattern is new in every moment
> And every moment is a new and shocking
> Valuation of all we have been.[8]

There will be a variety of groups in the new Church of the new age – discussion groups, action groups, prayer groups, groups of ministers and inter-disciplinary groups, local groups, national and international groups. Many will fail and fall apart, most will wax and wane, all will experience tension as well as joy, and each one will be a matrix where to a greater or lesser degree people may experience forgiveness and come alive with the life of the new age, and be a centre from which that life may spread into the community round about.

9. *The Community*

The third dimension in the style of the new Church is
community work. If the groups which we have described in
the last chapter are to enable the whole human race to
enter into the new age, then their life must spill over into
the community and set people free.

This setting free demands a change of attitude so simple
but so radical that when it is described people often nod
their heads as though it were obvious, but utterly fail
to understand because they have never experienced anything like it. The change is the change from paternalism to
interdependence. The purpose of community work is to
set people free to be responsible.

Perhaps I should begin with two stories, which illustrate a theory of community work expressed by Richard
Hauser in the diagram on p. 127.

He begins from where we are, in the urban society of
today with its twin characteristics of apathy and violence.
We take this apathy in its most hopeful manifestation,
which is curiosity – although I feel nothing can be done,
and that 'they' are all-powerful, at least I have within me
a natural curiosity (especially if I am young), and I wonder
within myself and imagine what it would be like if
something could be done. Similarly we take violence in
its most hopeful manifestation, which is indignation – I am
angry and frustrated, but have not yet reached that final
despair in which nothing is left for me to do except smash
the place up.

We then proceed to an action survey in which we try to
discover within a community what is the common point of
curiosity or the common point of indignation. As we question people, and encourage people to articulate their needs,

we ask them as our final question, 'Are you prepared to do anything about it?' From those who say 'yes' we assemble a group of potential leaders, who are ready to take action in a hopeful direction.

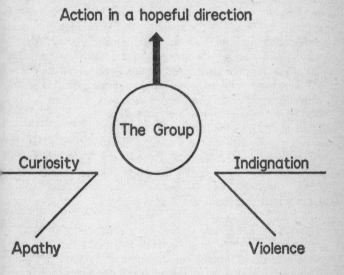

Action in a hopeful direction

The Group

Curiosity

Indignation

Apathy

Violence

Here are two stories from real life illustrating this theory. A common point of curiosity came to the surface in a suburb of Adelaide, in South Australia. We asked the people in the locality to tell us what were their social problems, and the most immediate one that came to mind was: 'Youth. Our young people. They are interested in nothing but cars, and spend their evenings just driving around.' So we gathered a group of young people, and asked them what they were really interested in. 'Cars,' they said, 'we are really interested in cars. We would love to have an old shed somewhere on a piece of waste land where we could take old cars to pieces and put them together again. Perhaps some friendly adult, who is a mechanic, might come and help us. Perhaps the garage down the road would let us have some old tools and old tyres.' Then, as they talked, enthusiasm grew, and they began to see how this shed could become a sort of youth centre, with one part of it walled off as a meeting-room and a coffee bar. 'We could show interesting films,' they said, 'and discuss them. We could think about some of the great world problems. And about what we ourselves want to do and to be.' Their common point of curiosity (which incidentally was a common point of indignation for the adults) had become the spring out of which was unleashed the whole creative longing of these young people to explore the world and to become responsible citizens in it. But as long as well-meaning adults opened youth clubs for them, only a few boys and girls responded, and these tended to be from the more intellectual or *status quo* families.

A common point of indignation burst out of a housing estate in Coventry, England. It had been built immediately after the war, in answer to the acute housing shortage, and before the days of social planning. It was a dismal place, from which over half the population was trying to escape, and into which gathered the 'problem families' of the city. The streets and grass verges were littered with rubbish – paper, tins, broken glass – and in the yards and alleyways were stacked old rusty bed-steads, broken tiles and junk. There was a church in the middle of the housing estate, which had been operating for fifteen years, but was attended only by a few loyal supporters.

We decided to invite to the vicarage half a dozen angry people, and we chose men and women who had written to the newspaper or voiced some other kind of protest. After talking together for about twenty minutes we had reached the 'common point of indignation'. 'This place is filthy,' they said.

'So what are you going to do about it?' we asked.

'*They* must do something. The Council House.' Then, after a few more minutes, 'No, *we* must do something. But we have no leaders.'

This was a critical moment. The vicar might have said, 'Brothers, I will be your leader.' But being a wise and umble man (Roy Boole is his name) he kept silent.

After a few minutes more, they began to look at each other, and to say, 'We could be the leaders – if we did it together.' So they began to plan a course of action. They canvassed their friends, and arranged a public meeting, and at that meeting I saw a man named Stan Reynolds, who had never done anything like this in his life before, grow into a chairman in half an hour. He began nervously, with his head down. Within half an hour, his chin was up, and he was calling the meeting to order, 'Shut up, Jo. Let Mrs Bullock speak.' The local councillor had come to the meeting, and being less wise than the vicar tried to take it over and make some political capital out of it. But the new action group was beginning to grow in self-confidence, and would not put themselves in his hands. They decided to send a demand to the Council House to clean up the place.

When the protest produced no result, they called upon the whole community to dump their rubbish in the streets so as to block them one Saturday morning. This was obviously a health hazard, and the Council had to send out rubbish disposal units and pay them overtime to clean the streets. The people on the housing estate had won a victory and began to see themselves with a new self-respect. They planned to form a tenants association, and invited over the chairman and secretary of a community group on a housing estate in another part of the city to learn how it could be done. When the association was launched, a third of the total population was enrolled into its membership in the first three months. They organized a sports day for the children and an outing for the Old Age Pensioners, and began to raise £12,000 to build a hut as a youth and community centre.

At about this time, one of the tutors in Social Science at the Lanchester Polytechnic in Coventry said to me, 'Very interesting, what's going on at Wood End. But surprising that the Church has had nothing to do with it.' That was the measure of our success. If the Church had been seen to be promoting it, or indeed had pushed it in any way, the venture would never have worked. Our role was first to enable it to happen, by giving people the opportunity to meet each other both within the housing estate and across the city, and then to support it, as the action group ran into difficulties.

For imperceptibly the action group slid into the role of 'them'. No longer was the whole population united against 'them', the bureaucrats in the Council House, but poor Stan himself, as he toiled around in a van collecting old newspapers to raise money for the community centre, asked one of his neighbours to help him carry a bundle out of his house to the van and was told 'Carry your own bloody papers.' Before long 'they', the action group, who had now become the committee of the tenants association, were being accused of fiddling the funds. The people had subscribed a few pennies for a few weeks, and there was no sign of the hut. What was happening?

Behind the scenes the committee were caught in a tangle of red tape. They were learning totally new skills – how to write letters to local government departments, how to apply for planning permission and for grants, how to get accounts audited. Our job was to encourage unobtrusively, and to persevere in the endless and essential function of arranging for people to meet each other. I remember one night when we arranged for the lady councillor, who was chairman of the education committee, and who happened to be a member of our congregation at the Cathedral, to meet with the committee of the tenants association at Wood End. The housing estate tenants had a fantasy that anyone working at the Council House was a hard-faced and steely-hearted bureaucrat. The Council House staff had a fantasy that the action group on the housing estate was composed of shaggy communist revolutionaries. When the charming, warm-hearted lady councillor met Stan and his colleagues and drank coffee with them, and discussed their project with an obvious appreciation of all they had done and enthusiasm for what they hoped to achieve next, you could almost hear the ice cracking.

Three years later, after I had left Coventry, I received an invitation to the opening of the Youth and Community Centre at Wood End. But this is not a success story. Like all other community work stories it was a mixture of success and failure, and if we were to try and measure its success we would look not so much at the eventual opening of a community centre, but at the growth of responsibility amongst the people of that housing estate. I have told the story at length because it is a case history in which we can see illustrated some of the principles of community work.

(a) *Setting free potential.* There is vast power locked away in any community of human beings. After the invasion of Czechoslovakia by Russian tanks, Edward Bond the playwright said to me, 'There is one thing stronger than a tank, and that is a human being.' Instead of complaining that people are apathetic, we should be helping them to contribute the fantastically rich resources and talents which are lying dormant within them. If people are not responsible, and not willingly carrying burdens for each other, they are only half alive. This applies first to the community worker, but if he is brave enough to be one step ahead, continually growing and exercising the kind of leadership we described in the last chapter, then he can help other people to grow and develop. He can help them to be open-minded to the possibility of change, to listen, to contribute ideas and skills, to be self-critical, to respect themselves and others, to interact, to take responsible decisions with other people, and in doing these things to satisfy their own deep need to be needed, and to grow into their own proper spiritual stature.

(b) *Helping people to help themselves.* This is not 'doing good to others' by which so many well-meaning people have in the past satisfied their own egos. We who work in the 'helping professions' have too often kept people dependent on us, and not allowed them to grow up. A community worker said to me once, 'I think you clergy sometimes do more harm than good', and what he meant was that by working day and night to help people a minister (or for that matter a social worker) may be keeping them as children, and denying them the right to be responsible. We all know the condescending voice which 'the worker' puts on as he or she talks to the 'old folk' while running their club for them. The old folk would be happier, and would create a better club, if they ran it for themselves, because they know better than the worker what they need and what they enjoy. They have more wisdom than he does, though they depend upon his support as their physical frailty increases, and upon his help to cope with a changing world which they do not easily understand. But if he 'does good to them', he drives them into senility.

(c) *Enabling people to meet each other*. This is probably the social need number one of our urban life. We are fragmented into class ghettos, and specialist work situations, within which we harbour fantasies about each other. We are hemmed into little individual houses or 'apartments', where father, mother and two kids are isolated from their neighbours and forced up against each other, with no escape to green fields or grandparents round the corner. It is necessary to meet each other across these boundaries if we are to grow into our true selves – to meet because we want to meet and have common interests and concerns. The problems of city life can only be solved if we get together and listen to each other – for example the problem of teenage crimes of violence cannot be solved by the police, but can and must be solved by all of us opening up together for the teenagers the rich opportunities of city life today.

(d) *Articulating needs and purposes*. As we have already seen, with reference to the Marketing Concept, advertising skill can be deployed in making people think they need what some manufacturer has to offer them. But even greater skill is needed to sort out and bring into consciousness what a society of complicated human beings actually needs. Maslow has suggested that there is a hierarchy of needs, which begin with the basic physical needs for food and shelter, and ascend through the social needs for belonging into the spiritual needs for self-fulfilment and self-transcendence.

The needs at the lower level, he suggests, have to be met before the higher needs can be acknowledged. When we have succeeded in articulating these complex needs of our society, then we are able to move on to the next difficult step, which is to frame a purpose and pursue it.

The community worker who involves himself in this process is playing with dynamite. If he invites people to express their needs and clarify their purposes, what guarantee has he that these needs and purposes will be beneficial? It is certain that good and evil will be interlocked, and that together with legitimate needs for human rights he will rouse up hatreds for past wrongs and prejudices against what is unfamiliar (such as foreigners), and the desire for scapegoats on to whom we can project what we dislike in ourselves. He may then find himself in a very awkward position. To those in authority he may appear as a danger-ous revolutionary stirring up trouble. To the people he may appear as a compromiser who lacks the courage of his convictions. We shall have to return to his predicament in a moment.

Meanwhile, we observe that community work of this kind is being practised in many fields. We quote examples from the fields of medicine, education and the arts.

A year or two ago I visited a special unit in a mental hospital, where the patients are encouraged to share with the staff in the responsibility of day-to-day decision-making. There are two group sessions each day, which the seventy to eighty people who make up the unit are encouraged to attend. On the morning I was present they were discussing the request of a patient that he be moved from one working section to another. I supposed that the chairman, who was handling this large group situation with great skill and com-posure, was the doctor in charge. During the discussion a big, rather untidy man came in late, and sat on a table. He spoke aggressively, banging on the table with his fist. After some forty minutes a well-dressed man, who had been listening intently but had not yet spoken, summed up the whole discussion in a few sentences, and proposed a solution which was immediately adopted. I took it that he must be the psychiatrist in charge of this particular case, and that the decision was a foregone conclusion after what had been only a charade. I was wrong in every case. The chairman and the man who summed up were both patients, and the untidy man whom I had supposed to be a rather disturbed patient turned out to be a male nurse. The doctors had been present, but had not spoken.

In the field of education the work of Paulo Freire has made an impact throughout the whole continent of South America. In his book *Pedagogy of the Oppressed,* he expounds a type of education which will set men free not only from their oppressors, but also from the egoism of their oppressors which sees everything as an object to be possessed. This kind of learning begins when the educator trusts the people, and no longer tries to fill them with information according to a programme which he himself has drawn up. He helps them to pose problems which arise out of the here and now of their own concrete situations, but always at the same time to commit themselves to action which emerges out of their reflection, because through this action they will clarify their understanding of the problem, and at the same time change themselves, and begin to believe in themselves. This new understanding will, in turn, reinvigorate their action, because 'the form of action men adopt is to a large extent a function of how they see themselves in the world.'

The method of this education is always dialogue, which cannot exist 'in the absence of a profound love for the world and for men . . . Love is at the same time the foundation of dialogue and dialogue itself.' 'Through dialogue, the teacher-of-the-students and the students-of-the-teacher cease to exist and a new term emerges: teacher-student with students-teachers.' This kind of dialogue cannot exist without humility. 'Someone who cannot acknowledge himself to be as mortal as everyone else still has a long way to go before he can reach the point of encounter.' It involves mutual trust, and hope, and a kind of critical thinking, 'which discerns an indivisible solidarity between the world and men admitting of no dichotomy between them – thinking which perceives reality as process and transformation, rather than as a static entity – thinking which does not separate itself from action, but constantly immerses itself in temporality without fear of the risks involved'. As they engage together in such dialogue and action, men and women become aware of their 'epoch' within the continuity of history. 'An epoch is characterized by a complex of ideas, concepts, hopes, doubts, values, and challenges in dialectical interaction with their opposites, striving towards fulfilment.' 'I consider the fundamental theme of our epoch,' writes Paulo Freire, 'to be that of *domination*. This implies that the objective to be achieved is *liberation*, its opposite theme.' He has proved again and again how this style of education can enable illiterate peasants to break through the accepted limits of their situation, and to open a way to a new future. Yet always as they learn, the illiterate peasants are teaching the teachers, and he quotes Guevara, who lived in a peasant community not only as a guerilla but also as a medical doctor, as saying, '*Communion with the people,* ceasing to be a mere theory, became an integral part of ourselves.' It was Guevara's humility, he continues, and his capacity to love that made possible his communion with the people, and enabled them to build out of their encounter with this revolutionary leader a theory of action, through which they could achieve freedom.[1]

It is in the field of art that many community movements have their origin. Studio Watts has developed in the black ghetto of Los Angeles where the racial riots took place in 1965. It began with a sculptor opening a studio, where young people were welcome to come and work but not to hang about. 'We realized as we talked with these young apprentices that it was what they saw happening that attracted them – a member of their community was offering himself as a resource to them.' Gradually training programmes were developed. 'The need of young people, particularly in low income communities, is not merely for community workshops. Rather, the need is for programmes that will provide them with an additional exposure to new environments, and to new ways of seeing and using the institutions, spaces and opportunities beyond the inner city.' Next, the plan extended to include children between the ages of two and five in an 'Environmental Pre-School', which would take the children (and if possible their parents) to different parts of the city and expose them 'to environments different from their own, and allow them to interpret and expand upon what they had experienced.' When Watts was designated as a community redevelopment area, Studio Watts urged that there should be community involvement and participation at all levels of planning, and offered an artist as an 'advocate planner' – as the link between community residents and designers. Through such involvement they believed they could 'unleash the community's psychic energies, to care enough and feel potent enough to make a living place of the new housing'. Then came the first street art festival, called the Chalk-In. 'Kids, teenagers, parents and professionals came to do chalk paintings on the blacktop street,' and a popular vote was taken and prizes were given. Out of the Chalk-In grew a photographic competition and a quarterly publication, dealing with local themes such as 'the matter of colour' and including poems from children. Then came the Los Angeles Festival of Performing Arts, which commissions three or four original works in drama, dance and music, to be performed by 'festival apprentices' under the direction of professionals. From this grew the 'Speak-Out', by which people were enabled to speak out, through drama, about their needs for companionship, for privacy, for security, and for spontaneity in their lives. As the centre continues to evolve it becomes possible to write, 'Studio Watts Workshop is a community arts institute. It is also a catalyst in a continuing effort to engage the urban dweller in the revitalizing of his community. In establishing Studio Watts Workshop we expressed our belief that the strength which an individual develops through participation in creative activity is a major force in the renewal of the city. Creativity is positive; through creation the individual can begin to recognize himself as a resource for his community's improvement. Through participation in arts programmes such as those developed and implemented by Studio Watts Workshop, he gains both a sense of himself, and another route to understanding his society and the ways in which he can use its resources.'[2]

Several such groups based on the arts have sprung up in London. 'Inter-Action' was established in 1968 'to make the arts more relevant to local community life', and to 'break down barriers of communication between traditionally juxtaposed elements such as teacher and pupil, actor and audience, amateur and professional, young and old'. Talented young actors are encouraged to work with young people, 'to involve them, wherever they usually congregate, in the basic idea of play, from play-group to play-making'. They 'provide a framework which will elicit creativity or participation on the part of others . . . This involvement is seen to be part of the artistic product. Thus the professional who enables young people to participate in or create a play is creating a new form of drama, one as relevant to our times as those we have inherited.' Ed Burman, the director, explains: 'We try to show the children that they themselves can create and gain a sense of personal worth that way. But the important thing is to set them a framework to demonstrate how every activity benefits from self-discipline.'[8]

Centreprise is in Hackney. But what is it? A bookshop, a coffee-bar, a meeting-room, an advice centre, a play-group, a play-bus, a people's newspaper, a street theatre? It is all these things and more. A community project, that channels professional advice to 'grass roots' groups who need help. A summer holiday camping scheme. An adventure playground. It started from a bookshop 'because there wasn't one in Hackney . . . and the sales show that people do need books – and personal service and time to ask and answer questions.' And it looks to the future: 'There are plans – for law clinics, vans to transport people to places, projects for other parts of the borough; there are all the things we want to publish by and about Hackney. There are masses of ideas about the arts.'[4]

This emphasis on the arts is significant. As the human race approaches the evolutionary leap forward in the realm of the spirit, we must expect that the flash-point of change will be that moment of self-awareness in which we can say, 'Aha, now I know what I am.' To bring us to this new awareness is the function of the artist.

What is the artist doing? In the first instance he is expressing his own feelings. Benjamin Britten in the *War Requiem* expresses his horror of old men who sacrifice the young in war, and his longing for the peace which springs from 'wells too deep for tears'. In order to express these feelings he has to pay attention to them, to focus upon them, to bring them up into consciousness, and this is a perilous and creative activity. He has to become self-conscious, to become aware of himself having contradictory feelings, for example, of terror and of pity. As an artist owns such feelings, as he brings them up into consciousness, he can convert them into imaginative ideas and express them in works of art which other people can see and hear.

So what he does primarily for himself, the artist is also doing for us. He is one step ahead of us. He is a brave and sensitive man who confesses to himself the secrets of his own heart, and who recognizes that good and evil are interlocked within him. He knows with Blake that:

Joy and woe are woven fine
A clothing for the soul divine,
Man was made for joy and woe
And when this we rightly know
Through the world we safely go.

He enables us to discover the secrets and the ambiguities of our hearts. But most of us do not want to know, which is why artists are generally rejected by the people of their own time. For example, a critic in 1804 wrote of Beethoven's second symphony, 'It is a crass monster, a hideously writhing wounded dragon.'[5] In 1823 another wrote of his seventh symphony, 'This is a composition in which the author has indulged a great deal of disagreeable eccentricity. Altogether it seems to have been intended as a kind of . . . hoax.'[6] What these critics are telling us is that they cannot and indeed dare not feel those emotions which Beethoven has expressed. That hideously writhing wounded dragon must be pushed back into the critic's subconscious, so that he may pretend for a few more years that the polite eighteenth century has not come to an end and that the French Revolution has not really happened.

We have to recognize the importance of what the artists are doing for us. The problem is that we only allow up into our consciousness those feelings of which we are not afraid. But there are other feelings of which we are very frightened, and they are like savage animals roaming and roaring about in the tangled forest of our unconscious. These we generally repress. We pretend they aren't there. We let up into our consciousness the tame cats but not the savage tigers, not the anger, or the feeling of our own helplessness, or the terrifying demands of compassion and holiness. So we corrupt our consciousness, for it tells us lies and not the truth, we corrupt the whole of our personal and social life, we corrupt our politics, we corrupt our theology. Feelings are the raw material of our thinking, and if we dare not feel honestly then we cannot think straight.[7]

Today, the community artists whom we have been describing are turning direct to the people and saying, 'Come and be artists with us.' They are telling us that to be an artist you do not need to become an aesthete who lives in a garret (any more than to be a contemplative you need to become a hermit who lives in a cave). Everyman can be an artist. Indeed, if we are to express the deep and powerful emotion which is struggling up into the consciousness of this generation, then perhaps everyman *must* be an artist, because it is an emotion which we shall have to express together. We might call this emotion compassion, and the imaginative idea into which we are converting it might be called complexity or interdependence, and the work of art which we are creating from it might be called the new age. But no. Not that! Not that! As we define these concepts they die on us, unless we translate them into action. Paulo Freire knows that his students will not understand a theory unless they are all the time testing it in action, and in the same way the true artist knows that he only becomes fully conscious of his imaginative idea in the act of painting it or sculpting it or writing it down. As the Irishman put it, 'I don't know what I think till I hear what I say.' A true work of art is not a cliché which the artist has in a plastic bag in the deep freeze of his memory, and which he can bring out and cook up and feed to an audience at will. It is always original, always being born out of the present moment, and always in danger of being rejected by the majority of mankind because it reveals to us more about ourselves than we are ready to acknowledge.

So we are led back to the predicament of the community worker, for it is beginning to look as if he must be something of an artist, and as though this operation on which he is engaged will turn out in practice to be highly dangerous. People are dynamite, and if they really meet each other then we can expect trouble, for not only creative potentialities may be released but also fear, jealousy and prejudice. If he reveals to them the secrets of their hearts, or even begins to draw away the veil, he will provoke irrational anger. The storm breaks over him, and if he is a faulty lightning conductor he is destroyed. It is absolutely necessary, if he is to do community work, that he should understand the forces which are operating around him. He must understand how groups in society interact with other groups, what fantasies different professions or classes have about each other, and what difficulties there are in communicating from one group to another – both of articulating what our own group wants to say, and also of hearing what the other group is trying to say to us. He must understand how people react to each other within the same group – their ambiguous love and fear of each other, their ambiguous need for, and hostility to, authority, and how those in authority are flattered by this need and threatened by this hostility. He must understand himself, because the forces operating in society also operate within himself, and if he doesn't recognize this he will be torn to pieces.

He must, therefore, be a member of a group, who will support him and help him to understand the contradictions by which he is being buffeted, and who will go on believing in him when he makes mistakes. But there is one thing more to say. The interlocking of good and evil in society can only be transformed by death and resurrection. It may be that calamity has to strike a community before responsibility to each other can be reborn, or it may be that the costly work of suffering and healing has to be done by someone or by a group of people before the new order with its new quality of interdependence can appear. This may be the vocation of the community worker – not the end which he deliberately seeks in a mood of masochism, but the high calling which seeks for him, and which in the end he has to fulfil.

Such a group, having death and resurrection as the essential rhythm of its life, exists already in nearly every community in the world. I mean, of course, the Christian Church. Potentially, it is the ferment of the new life. Its vocation, in the most profound sense, is community work. Its mission is to set people free – to enable them to become their true selves, to be responsible for each other, and to respond to the divine purpose. Its destiny is to bear within itself, at this time of crisis on 'spaceship earth', the mystery of the death of Jesus, and his risen life which is the life of the new age.

10. *St George and the Dragon*

'That's all cloud-cuckoo-land,' said a minister of religion, when a few years ago I first tried to outline this threefold pattern of renewal at a clergy conference. It seemed to him totally unrealistic, in comparison with the actual situation in the institutional Churches up and down the country. But since then the mood has changed and the renewal has gathered impetus. Today we are faced with the question, 'What is the relation of the institutional Church to this renewal, which appears to be happening on its periphery, or outside it altogether?'

Many who are involved in the renewal movements are tempted to say, 'We must break away from the institutional Church – the Spirit is moving elsewhere.' But this would probably be a mistake, for we can see from past history that break-away sects have usually ended up by becoming institutions themselves. We need an institutional Church, and if we destroy one we have to create another.

(1) We need it because of our weakness. All our life long there remains within us the dependent child. We sin. We face death. In these moments of weakness we need to be carried, to hear the words of unconditional forgiveness spoken objectively, and to be confronted by the mercy which spans the centuries.

(2) We need it to express our unity, not only with all Christians and all men now living, but also with our ancestors and with future generations. Through the institutional Church, its architecture, its history, its art, its prayers, we can receive from our ancestors their faith, their human weakness and their sense of divine love. They can flow into us, and we in turn can hand on ourselves to our descendants, so that past, present and future may be gathered into one – one

movement, one stillness – in which we may know the timeless presence.

(3) We need it for the study of theology, and for the training of leaders who will pass on the Christian story and symbols to the next generation, so that they in their turn may be able to receive them, break them and rediscover them.

But always alongside the institution we need the renewal movement. Parallel with the Church which hands on 'the Faith', we need a para-church where little companies of people risk living together in the interaction of faith.

The Christian must be prepared to stand with one foot in the institution and the other in the renewal movement, and to suffer the contradictions between them. As Dr A. M. Ramsey said, while he was Archbishop of Canterbury, it is the duty of the institution 'to serve these little companies of love and faith'. Equally, the institution needs them, if it is to grow and change and be transformed under the direction of the Spirit. The Companies, for their part, need the institution, to rebel against, to return to when they have got lost, and to keep them in dialogue with people whose understanding of the truth is different from their own.

One of the traditional functions of the institution has been to guard against heresy. The word heresy means 'a part of the truth', which is so over-emphasized that it neglects other elements and becomes 'a perversion of the truth'. Heresy has been a recurrent danger of the renewal movement over the centuries, and at this moment we have continually to be reminding ourselves that the way of renewal is a threefold way. We have called the three dimensions of this way contemplation, the group, and community work. If any one of these three dimensions of renewal is practised without the other two, it becomes a perversion. Contemplation becomes a retreat into unreality, because a man cannot grow to know God unless at the same time he is growing to know himself, and he cannot come to a knowledge of himself except through knowing others. The group becomes an introverted huddle, exaggerating the neuroses of its members, unless it recognizes itself as the channel through which the divine love can flow into the community round about. Community work becomes activism, which may destroy the community it is trying to serve, unless the community worker is continually growing in sensitivity towards people, and in the clarification of the divine purpose. One alone is a heresy – but so are any two which neglect the third. The way is essentially three in one; but at the same time it is one in three, for through each and all of its three aspects it leads towards a single knowledge of good and evil interwoven through the whole texture of our lives, interlocked in the heights and depths of our experience, and only to be transformed through death and resurrection.

What do we mean by death and resurrection? We appear to be using the words in two different senses. First to describe those occasions in our lives which may be frequently repeated, and which Jesus seems to imply should be experienced daily, when we have to give up something we hold dear and come to a deeper orientation of our own self-consciousness. Secondly, to describe physical death, such as the death of Jesus on the cross, and a subsequent resurrection to eternal life. What justification is there for using the same words to describe such disparate events?

If we return to the myth of the Holy Grail, we see the first kind of 'death' in the moment at which Perceval's sword broke in the fight with Orguelleus. He had to discover that the very best thing in him was also the very worst – that his pride in being a Knight of the Round Table was the cause both of his venturing out and persevering in his search for the Holy Grail, and also of his being unable to find it. Only after the symbol of his knightly prowess had been shattered was he ready and humble enough to become the guardian of the Grail. This was his 'resurrection'. But if he had been humble from the start, he would never have set out. There had to be pride, and there had to be the death of pride, before resurrection could be realized.

Along the journey of contemplation we arrive at the same crux. The contemplative becomes aware that 'the grace is

upon me', and this is at the same time God's truth and
the devil's opportunity. If he lingers here he is in danger of
taking himself too seriously and becoming aggressive, and
then his spiritual pride pollutes the river of grace which
flows through him. He has to go out into the desert, and
be no longer aware that he is aware of grace.

> . . . In order to arrive there,
> To arrive where you are, to get from where you are not,
> You must go by a way wherein there is no ecstasy.[1]

He has to become humble, earthy. To break the image
which has brought him so far on his way. Perhaps to give
up what he has understood to be prayer ('Whatever you do,
don't pray') and simply to hold the hand of someone he
loves in a bewildered silence, or to go and play with a child.

In the life of a group we are brought again and again
to this same painful point of self-knowledge. The very
thing which I had known to be my strength is suddenly
shown to be my weakness. Light shines in the darkness. A
new area of my unconscious life is brought up into consciousness and I am confronted by my own ambiguity. I
am unmasked in my own sight. Generally this would not have
happened – I would not have allowed this self-knowledge
to slip through my defences – except in the company of
people whom I can trust and who accept me as I am. Because
they are holding me together, I can allow myself to fall apart
and to be creatively remade. (This *should* be the normal
pattern in a group where there is wise leadership, and
which is founded on the forgiveness of Christ. It is very
difficult to force anyone into self-knowledge – he simply
will not hear what is being said. Generally he will only accept
self-knowledge when he is ready for it, and when there are
sympathetic people to help him cope with it. But there are
ambiguities in every human group, and we can sometimes
help a person to a moment of self-knowledge by a friendship
which does not go deep enough to support him through it, or
at a moment when it may not be possible to continue sup-

porting him. This can be very dangerous and damaging.)

In the process of community work we arrive at a similar point of 'death' which is often described as disillusion. The people will not respond. They are willing enough to accept any benefits we can win for them, but when there is work to be done or things go badly they turn against us. Depths of prejudice, dishonesty and jealousy are revealed. But in whom are they revealed? In the people, yes, but also in the community worker. 'After all I have done for them,' he says – and that lets the cat out of the bag, or should we say the tiger out of the unconscious? Why was I doing this community work? Was it because of a deep need in myself to be appreciated, a deep sense of insecurity, a fear – a panic – that I am not loved? I am disillusioned, because the truth is breaking through my self-esteem and showing up the ambivalence of my motives. The people, too, are disillusioned. They had looked for easy results, but now uncomfortable demands are being made. They had an image of themselves as kind neighbours . . . but now? 'That half-way house for men coming out of prison, to help them find their feet, we don't want it in *our* street, thank you. Our children would be raped and murdered.' So the people, too, find their pretences swept away. In this moment of truth, if the truth is too painful to bear, they may turn nasty and lash out at the community worker (the politician?, the prophet?) who has disturbed their peace. Or alternatively, having brought some deep-seated prejudice into the light, they may be able to deal with it positively – to discover, perhaps, that they too are criminals only they have not yet been found out, that they too are in prison only the prison bars are their own fears, and that now if they can welcome the ex-prisoners into their street, they will in this very act of acceptance be setting themselves free. As for the community worker, he may discover that the need in himself which drove him into community work has been all the time the flaw in his personality which has made that work ineffective. Now, if he can accept it, laugh with himself about it, and use it to understand the needs of others, his weakness will be transformed into his strength.

If these examples help us to understand the nature of 'death and resurrection' in our daily lives, then I believe we can go on to say that physical death, and resurrection to eternal life, are the ultimate event in the same series.

When my wife was dying, if I may be forgiven once more for being personal, it was as though the light was being let into the darkness, so that it illuminated the good and evil at the roots of our personalities, both mine and hers. With her it happened over the last months. She became, in the true sense of the word, disillusioned, so that she faced her own ultimate fear and recognized her own inherent beauty – so that she passed beyond the awareness of her awareness of God, and saw with clarity and compassion into the lives of those who came to visit her. It was as though a great work was being done through her. When we came upon these words of Julian of Norwich, she said, 'Yes, that's it.'

> The Lord showed me that a great work would be done,
> and that he himself would do it,
> and that I would do nothing but sin,
> but that my sinning would not hinder his goodness working.

The work was the work of letting the light into the darkness. As she walked deeper into that darkness, so the light penetrated with her, till it shone through her weakness into the ultimate darkness of death. It was as though, through suffering, she brought up into consciousness the sin and pain which was in herself and in the world around her, so that it could be accepted and transformed. It was as though the 'great work' which the Lord himself was doing, and which she did not hinder, was the work of redeeming the world.

For me, too, her death was a time of painful disillusion. The words which came alive to me in the days that followed were the words of St Paul. 'The sting of death is sin, and the strength of sin is in the law.' The ultimate failure to be your true self, the ultimate failure of responsibility and faith, these are only shown up by the death of the one you love. Through what death did St Paul pass to experience that sting of sin, and to learn that all the laws of God and man had only made his sin stronger? His strength, his Pharisaic religion, had been his fatal weakness. But you can only accept that unmasking of your hypocrisy – that new depth of self-knowledge – when *the death of the one you love is also the death of the one who loves you*. Then the light which pierces into the ambiguity of your heart is not the light of criticism but the light of unambiguous love, which shows you that you are already accepted, and that your weakness, once recognized, is your strength. 'Death is swallowed up in victory,' writes St Paul. 'Thanks be to God, who gives us the victory through our Lord Jesus Christ.'

In Jesus is focused the whole truth of death and resurrection. On Good Friday the light shone into the darkness, exposing the ambiguity of all political and religious institutions and the good and evil interlocked at the roots of human personality. Jesus, as a great artist, brought up into consciousness the secrets of his own heart. He met his own ultimate weakness, uncovered the depths of suffering, and knew the absence of God. But through that weakness the light shone and penetrated into the darkness of death, so that the frontier between life and death was illuminated and revealed as the frontier between death and life. The divine love was being made perfect in weakness, and the divine compassion through suffering. As we remember that timeless moment, *first it is me and him* – the one whom I love has died, I am a sinner, Jesus, have mercy. *Then it is him and me* – the one who loves me has died, he has broken through the prison bars and is setting me free, in his great love he has broken through the gates of hell, Jesus, mercy. *Then it is only him* – he is alive, he is saying, 'Do not cling to me', go and be merciful (how happy are the merciful), go and tell all men about repentance, and test out in action the sovereign forgiveness of the new age.

What do we mean by the new age? Here again we seem to be using the words in two senses. First to describe any historical era, such as the Renaissance, which follows upon an 'evolutionary leap', when after a long period of gestation men and women emerge into a new understanding of 'what they are', and this self-understanding leads to an overall change in their institutions and ways of life. Secondly, to describe the new era which Jesus declared to be 'at hand' and which he called the kingdom of God. We can never say of this kingdom, 'Such and such a group of people, or I myself, have finally entered this new age.' It is a way to be walked each day. Its life is the divine Spirit flowing through human flesh, and this Spirit is always being given and received through the interaction of faith with the risen Christ. Again we have to ask, 'What justification is there for using the same words, the new age, to describe these different kinds of era?' The first are a series of historical eras which succeed one another in time. The second is a supra-historical era, which breaks into time through the here and now of any present moment.

The key lies in the ultimate term. In the discussion of death and resurrection, the ultimate term is the death and resurrection of Jesus, and it illumines all the others. Standing at that point, looking out from that perspective at our other deaths and resurrections, we can see the inner meaning which they carry, and what it is which they have it in them to achieve. So here in our discussion of the new age, the ultimate term is the kingdom of God – the divine love ruling through our self-knowledge and compassion. As we look back from this perspective over the 'new ages' of human history we can see what it is that entitles them to be so called. An overall change in human affairs which is in the direction of complexity and love can be called a 'new age' – for example, the Renaissance. An overall change which is in the opposite direction cannot be called a new age – for example, the rise of Nazism in Germany. A 'new age' partakes of the ultimate character of the kingdom of God.

We could argue that this is difficult to assess. Good and

evil are interlocked. The Renaissance freed us from the hierarchies of the Middle Ages, but enslaved us to other and perhaps more savage masters. Who is to say that the kingdom of God was advanced? May it not be that as one age succeeds another the sum of good and evil remains constant, and is only redistributed?

Yes, it may be so. But the ambiguity of good and evil can be transformed by death and resurrection. This truth is focused in – though it is not monopolized by – the death and resurrection of Jesus, through which unambiguous love is set free. Any historical age can rightly be called a 'new age' if it sets free the spring of divine love in the hearts of men and women, and if it gives birth to new structures which allow the pattern of death and resurrection to be more continually experienced.

What, then, of Christ's Church? Is it too much to hope that, in this crisis of human history as we approach the evolutionary leap and the catastrophe locked together within the same events, that the Church can demonstrate the way of death and resurrection? Can she give a lead, by being one step ahead? Can she both recognize within herself the interlocking of good and evil, and experience day by day the death and resurrection by which they are transformed?

It is cloud-cuckoo-land to expect that the institutional Church will suddenly become totally Christ-like. By its very nature as a human institution, it is and will always remain ambiguous. But the institutional Church in the shape we have known it is changing. Economically, it is becoming impossible to maintain the present structure of manpower and ecclesiastical buildings. Within a decade there will almost certainly be a drastic reduction in the number of full-time ministers of religion. If we look at these facts with eyes which are open to the pattern of death and resurrection, we may see through this 'death' into a time of rebirth, when a greater measure of responsibility will be shared by the laity, and when the typical meeting of Christians will become once again the small group eating a meal together in a house.

It is not cloud-cuckoo-land to hope, on the evidence of what is now happening, that in every place there may emerge a small group of people whose life demonstrates the threefold pattern of renewal. But we shall have to be careful that such groups, engaged in contemplation and community work, do not fool themselves into supposing that they have at last discovered the ultimate shape of the Christian Church. Not that! Not that! This new structure will be as ambiguous as the old. It too must die, indeed death is written into its very constitution, for no group will be able to follow this threefold pattern of renewal without coming up against the frequent experience of death. Essentially it is not a structure but a way, a way which expresses itself through the rhythm of birth and death and resurrection, a way in which travellers will come to the top of a ridge only to see the higher mountain ranges unfolding beyond. It is a perilous journey, the way of disillusion, only to be embarked upon by groups of people who are prepared to take risks and to make mistakes and to go on forgiving each other; and yet it is not so perilous as to stand still, because only 'on the way' will be the one who says, 'I am the Way.'

So what I foresee, or at least hope for, is an institutional Church and parallel with it a para-church. The dividing line will not run between us, so that some of us are in one and some of us in the other, but it will run through the middle of each of us so that all of us are in both.

The institutional Church will represent stability, and the mercy of God spanning the centuries. It will be located in centres of excellence, such as cathedrals and universities and international centres of research, where theology will be studied, music and the arts will find their natural home, leaders will come for training, and dialogue will take place between men and women of different races, faiths and professions. It will have a second tier in geographical areas, such as a town with its surrounding villages or an urban borough (an Anglican rural deanery or a Methodist district) where the laity will come for celebrations, for training in the faith and in prayer and in pastoral counselling, and for the exploration of local concerns such as health, industry, education, and politics. It will have a third tier at the level of the parish, where the local Christians will be both the para-church and the institutional Church and will meet in both styles.

The para-church will represent growth and change, and the presence of God in the here and now. It will be located in every sort of natural community and at every level, both in the geographical communities of the village, the block of flats, the town, the city, the conurbation, the continent, the world, and in the communities of common interest such as are formed by work, recreation, the arts, youth, and old age. It will take the form of the group, typically of the small group, and will be marked by spontaneity. Each group will follow the threefold pattern of renewal, though with differences in the emphasis which they place on each strand within the pattern. Above all, no two groups will be the same.

This institutional Church and this para-church will need each other, and will be constantly having to dispel the fantasies which they have about each other. This should not be impossible once everybody recognizes that he is in both. The leaders in these two styles of Church life, whether ordained ministers or lay men and women, will have a crucial task as interpreters and enablers, and they will recognize that they themselves need to be involved in a process of training and ongoing learning from the time of appointment to the time of retirement. They will need to keep one step ahead.

Finally, the relation will become clearer between the language of theology, and the language of poetry and myth. God cannot be confined within any language, so that in the end we have to fall silent in his presence. But the language of poetry and myth can at least point towards the mystery of his being, while the language of theology can control the poetry and the myth, not automatically, but in much the same way as the institutional Church serves the para-church. Theology will say to poetry and myth, 'You are going astray.

That is heresy, because you are over-emphasizing one part of the truth.' And in the end theology will have the last word, because when poetry and myth have done their best, it will say, 'Not that! Not that!'

Knowing, then, the danger, and that when we have written it down it will be inadequate, we will end with a myth. We began with the search for the Holy Grail, and we will end with St George and the dragon, for England needs her patron saint as never before.

Historically little is known about St George. He is said in the earliest records to have been a Roman soldier who lived somewhere in the Middle East, and was martyred for his Christian faith about AD 300. Presumably, like other Christians he refused to burn incense to the Roman emperor.

The Roman emperor was the head of state of the most powerful political institution that mankind had ever known. Within it good and evil were interlocked. Its armies and its laws had imposed peace, its engineers had built cities, roads, aqueducts, and they, together with its statesmen, poets and philosophers, had created a civilization which still influences our thinking and way of life today. But it had come to depend upon a system of slavery in which the slave, having no rights, could be flogged or killed at the whim of his master, and by the year AD 300 it had grown rotten with an inner corruption. When the Christians were asked to burn incense to the emperor, and so to recognize him as a god, they were being required to perform a ritual act which sophisticated people would not take very seriously, but which in general pledged their loyalty to the Roman system.

George and his fellow Christians found themselves in a situation of 'dissonance'. 'No,' they said, 'we will not burn incense. We have experienced a new quality of life which is based on freedom and compassion. We have been grasped by the truth of Christ, which it is now impossible for us to deny. We choose rather to die.' So they were arrested, and on the next public holiday they were brought to the arena and torn to pieces by wild animals.

That was the end of them. Or was it? A generation later

the emperor of Rome had become a Christian, and the new age of Christendom had begun. Was it the wild beast who had killed George, or George who through his dying had struck a blow which had transformed the wild beast?

So, we come to the dragon.

A dragon is a mythical creature, who has never existed anywhere on earth but is found as a universal symbol in human culture. He is a reptile with wings, who breathes fire, and who sits guarding hidden hoards of treasure. In China the dragon is generally benign. Sometimes he represents the rain god who sends the precious rain needed by the crops but who, when he is angry, sends storms and floods Sometimes he represents the emperor and his immediate family. Sometimes he represents wisdom, the guardian of the law who grasps within his paws the pearl of truth – one originally hostile dragon submitted to Buddha and became the guardian of the pearl of faith. In Chaldaea the dragon Tiamat represented the original chaos which was vanquished by the god Marduk, and was cut in half in an act of creation which separated the heaven and the earth. In Egypt Apophis, the great serpent of the world of darkness, was conquered by Ra. In Greece the dragons (*drakontes,* seeing with sharp sight) were generally beneficent powers, dwellers in the inner parts of the earth, wise to discover its secrets and to utter oracles. In Rome the *immanissimus draco* (the very inmost, immanent dragon) was the kindly representative of the *bona dea* (the good goddess, the mother of fruitfulness). In Britain the dragon appeared as the emblem of Uther Pendragon, who reigned immediately before King Arthur – he had two golden dragons made, one of which was dedicated in the cathedral at Winchester and the other carried with the army into battle.

This mysterious dragon, this serpent with wings, is the symbol of ourselves – of man in his undifferentiated state, man who is both animal and divine, a part of the reality which is nature/man/God. In the darkness of man's unconscious there roar savage beasts breathing fire, but there also broods a supernatural wisdom. If this chaos can be differentiated, this primeval darkness pierced with light, this unconscious brought up into consciousness, then the dragon will deliver up his hidden treasure. The dragon breathing fire will be transformed, so that he is no longer the irrational compulsion which drives and tosses and buffets us about, but the spirit of wisdom which is present both in the cathedral and in the battle. The treasure (the object of our desire) will be seen no longer as heaps of gold and precious stones, but as the pearl of faith for which a man would gladly sell everything else that he possesses.

The Hebrew Bible opens with the myth of God overcoming chaos. 'The earth was without form and void, and darkness was over the face of the deep, and the Spirit of God was brooding over the face of the waters.' Then God said, 'Let there be light.' The light penetrated into the darkness, and heaven was differentiated from earth, dry land from sea, day from night. Then God formed out of the chaos the fishes, the animals, the birds, each after his kind, and finally man made in his own image. For a timeless moment we see paradise, nature/man/God in perfect harmony, and man's true self, Adam/Eve/God living together in love and obedience. But there comes the serpent, more subtle than all the other animals for he is the serpent in the depths of man's consciousness, a reptile who aspires to divinity, who says, 'Eat of the tree and you shall be as gods, knowing good and evil.' So they eat, and the innocent childlike harmony of paradise is broken. They become self-conscious and hide their sexuality from each other with fig leaves, and they hide from God as he walks through the garden in the cool of the evening and calls, 'Adam, where art thou?' Adam and Eve are exiled from paradise, and they and their children become little isolated independent egos who defraud and oppress and kill each other through the long age which follows – the age of the knowledge of good and evil interlocked in the heart of man, the age of ambiguity and of the dragon.

The Christian gospels tell the story of how God acts again within the consciousness of man as he had originally acted in the creation of the physical world, how he overcomes the chaos and differentiates one thing from another. The Son of Man is the light shining in the darkness. He is the word of God piercing into the ambiguity of our hearts and minds, the truth of God piercing our illusions. But always and above all he is the love of God which does not judge and does not kill, but by his own death and resurrection brings up into consciousness the secrets of our hearts, and transforms the raw material of our being and sets us free.

Why then does St George, in Christ's name, kill the dragon? This is the tragic error which the generality of Christians fell into because they could not tolerate their own ambiguity – they projected the evil in themselves on to the world outside and then tried to kill it. True, the world was ambiguous and the life of the risen Christ was unambiguous. But it did not follow that paganism was darkness and they were light, or that the old dragons of paganism were evil and must be slain. *In trying to slay the dragon they were attempting the impossible because they were trying to do away with the instinctive, emotional, undifferentiated raw material of their own nature.* They succeeded only in driving it back into the subconscious whence it broke out again in irrational violence. The Crusaders saw the Saracens as evil and themselves as good, and this gave them a licence to plunder and destroy, and to vent upon others the punishment for the evil they dared not acknowledge and feel in themselves. It was the Crusaders who brought back St George from the Middle East to England and adopted him as their patron saint.

Uccello, painting in the fifteenth century as the Middle Ages passed into the Renaissance, expresses a deeper, truer insight in his picture of St George and the dragon which hangs in the National Gallery in London. On the left of the picture is a maiden chained to a dragon, but the curious thing which strikes you as you look more closely is that this maiden has the dragon on a chain. She is not chained to the dragon, but the dragon is chained to her like some kind of lapdog. Then you notice that the dragon's face, in spite of its fangs, is full of kindness and wisdom together with the agony of suffering caused by St George's blow. The long spear has pierced its eye, and as you trace back the line of the spear you see at the top right-hand corner of the picture, in the clouds behind St George, the eye of God. God is looking through St George's eye, down the spear, and into the dragon's eye. St George is piercing the dragon with the truth of God, or more exactly the truth of God is piercing the dragon through St George. The dragon is human nature, the dark, chaotic, undifferentiated raw material of the Roman Empire or of the fifteenth century or of the twentieth century, the illusion to which we are chained — or is it chained to us? As St George strikes there is terror and fire, blood and agony. Then, only a maiden and a soldier, and somebody's eye contemplating them.

The truth with which God strikes us is the divine love, which pierces our darkness through the death and resurrection of the Christ.

When St George pierced the dragon, in Christ's name, it was George who died and entered into the communion of saints, and the dragon who was transformed, and a new age which began.

Notes

2. THE CATASTROPHE

1. I owe this explanation of the Marketing Concept to Kenneth Adams, Director of Studies at St George's House, Windsor.

3. THE EVOLUTIONARY LEAP

1. *Behind Appearance: A Study of the Relations between Painting and Natural Sciences in this Century*, Edinburgh University Press, 1970.
2. Luke 9:23-5.
3. Luke 23:5.
4. John 14:6.

4. THE CHRIST

1. See Mark 1:14, 15.
2. Matthew 13:44.
3. John 13:34.
4. Matthew 18:23-35.
5. Mark 2:27.
6. Matthew 6:33.
7. Luke 17:24-5.
8. See Matthew 22:37-40.
9. Mark 1:22.
10. Mark 1:11-13.
11. John 2:4.
12. Matthew 10:5f.
13. Matthew 15:21-8.
14. Matthew 10:29.
15. Matthew 6:29.
16. Matthew 5:3.
17. John 4:5-26.
18. See C. H. Dodd, *Interpretation of the Fourth Gospel*, Cambridge University Press, 1953, pp. 144-50.
19. John 7:38.
20. The Greek word for belly (*koilia*) can also mean womb. It is the place of emotion, but also of rebirth.
21. T. S. Eliot, *Four Quartets*, 'Burnt Norton', I.
22. Mark 2:3-12.
23. Matthew 6:12-15.

5. DEATH AND RESURRECTION

1. Harry Williams in a lecture, 'The Church as an instrument for Change', March 1973.
2. *The Comedy of Dante Alighieri: Paradise,* translated by Dorothy L. Sayers and Barbara Reynolds, Canto XXXI, 11. 91-3, Penguin Books, 1962.
3. W. B. Yeats.
4. St Francis, 'Canticle of the Sun'.
5. *The Comedy of Dante Alighieri: Paradise,* op. cit., Canto XXXIII, 11. 139-45.
6. John 16:6-7.
7. Luke 24:47.
8. Luke 15:7.

INTERLUDE: THE SPRING OF LOVE

1. David L. Edwards, *Religion and Change,* Hodder & Stoughton, 1969, p. 325.
2. For the ideas and quotations in this paragraph, see John Platt, *Perception and Change,* University of Michigan Press, 1970, pp. 119-59.
3. Alexander Solzhenitsyn, *The First Circle,* Fontana, 1970, pp. 444, 160 and 390.
4. Isaiah 53:3-5.
5. Oxford Book of Sixteenth-Century Verse, p. 428.
6. Ibid., p. 431.
7. Luke 21:25-8.
8. Mark 13:8.
9. William Shakespeare, *Twelfth Night,* act 2, scene 3.
10. Piet Hein, *More Grooks,* Hodder & Stoughton, 1969, p. 16.
11. Luke 4:1.

7. CONTEMPLATION

1. Gerard Manley Hopkins.
2. T. S. Eliot, op. cit., 'Little Gidding', V.
3. George Herbert, 'The Temper', I.
4. T. S. Eliot, op. cit., 'Little Gidding', V.
5. Ibid.
6. John 12:24.

8. THE GROUP

1. Alfred, Lord Tennyson.
2. T. S. Eliot, op. cit., 'Little Gidding', V.
3. T. S. Eliot, op. cit., 'East Coker', II.

9. THE COMMUNITY

1. Paulo Freire, *Pedagogy of the Oppressed*, Penguin Books, 1972, pp. 62, 53, 63, 64-5, 73, 75, 138.
2. From a report, 'Studio Watts', Los Angeles, California.
3. From *The Times Educational Supplement*, 26 September 1969.
4. From a brochure, 'What is Centreprise?'
5. *Zeitung für die Elegente Welt*, Vienna, May 1804.
6. The Harmonicon, London, August 1823. These two quotations are taken from the *Lexicon of Musical Invective*, Nicolas Slonimsky, University of Washington Press, 1969, pp. 42-4.
7. See R. G. Collingwood, *The Principles of Art*, Oxford University Press, 1938.

10. ST GEORGE AND THE DRAGON

1. T. S. Eliot, op. cit., 'East Coker', III.